Lizard Island

SCIENCE AND SCIENTISTS ON AUSTRALIA'S GREAT BARRIER REEF

Sneed B. Collard III

Franklin Watts
A Division of Grolier Publishing
New York • London • Hong Kong • Sydney
Danbury, Connecticut

✻ To Erica, Brant, Eliza, and Alexandra, ✻
who help me find my land legs

Map by Bob Italiano
Interior design by Molly Heron

Photographs ©: Animals Animals: 25 (P. Parks/OSF); Archive Photos: 123 (Reuters/HO); BBC Natural History Unit: 82 (David Hall); Earth Scenes: 126 (Laurence Gould/OSF); Peter Arnold Inc.: 16 (Kelvin Aitken); Photo Researchers: 24 (A. Flowers & L. Newman), 54 right (David Hall), 54 left, 89 (Fred McConnaughey); Sneed B. Collard III: 45, 49, 51, 71 bottom, 72 top (David Bellwood), 108 (Julian Caley), 107 (P. Munday), 103, 109, 110 top (Lyle Vail), 113 (Dirk Zeller), cover, 14, 19, 23, 31, 34, 36, 43, 59, 63, 65, 66, 67, 68, 69, 70, 71 top, 72 bottom, 73, 77, 79, 85, 92, 95, 96, 105, 106, 110 bottom, 111, 112, 117.

Visit Franklin Watts on the Internet at:
http://publishing.grolier.com

Library of Congress Cataloging-in-Publication Data

Sneed, Collard B.
    Lizard Island: science and scientists on Australia's Great Barrier Reef / Sneed B. Collard III.
        p. cm.
    Includes bibliographical references and index.
    Summary: Describes the biologists who do work at the Lizard Island Research Station and their activities studying and protecting the Great Barrier Reef.
    ISBN 0-531-11719-7 (lib. bdg.)   0-531-16519-1 (pbk.)
    1. Coral reef ecology—Research—Australia—Lizard Island (Qld.)—Juvenile literature. 2. Coral reefs and islands—Research—Australia— Lizard Island (Qld.)—Juvenile literature. 3. Biologists—Biography—Juvenile literature. 4. Lizard Island Research Station (Qld.)— Juvenile literature. 5. Biologists. [1. Coral reef ecology. 2. Coral reefs and islands. 3. Lizard Island Research Station (Qld.). 4. Ecology.] I. Title.

QH197.C63   2000
577.7'89476—dc21   99-055149

GROLIER
PUBLISHING

9002000027310I

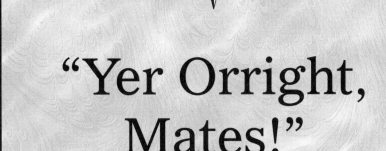

"Yer Orright, Mates!"

ONE OF THE DELIGHTS IN WRITING THIS BOOK WAS MEETING THE many friendly people who shared their knowledge and resources with me. I could never have even attempted this project without their support, enthusiasm, generosity, and encouragement. I'd like to especially thank the LIRS directors, Anne Hoggett and Lyle Vail, who were helpful from the very start and provided me with the vast majority of contacts I needed. I'd also like to give special credit to my editor Melissa Stewart, who suggested this great idea to me, and to my publisher John Selfridge, who got behind this project 100 percent. Now, to the list of "stars":

Michael Arvedlund, James Cook University
David Bellwood, James Cook University
Julian Caley, James Cook University
Brooke Carson-Ewart, The Australian Museum
John Howard Choat, James Cook University
Barry Duncan, Reef HQ (formerly The Great Barrier Reef Aquarium)

Jason Elliott, James Cook University

Alexandra Grutter, University of Queensland

Amanda Hay, Macquarie University

Andrew Heyward, Australian Institute of Marine Science

Polly and Mark Hilder, University of Tasmania

Anne Hoggett, Lizard Island Research Station

Susie Holst, James Cook University

Paul Hough, Reef HQ (formerly The Great Barrier Reef Aquarium)

Terry Hughes, James Cook University

Martin Jones, Reef HQ (formerly The Great Barrier Reef Aquarium)

The Kerr family, Cape Hillsborough

Brigid Kerrigan, James Cook University

Jeff Leis, The Australian Museum

Michael Marnane, James Cook University

Mark McCormick, James Cook University

Philip Munday, James Cook University

Andrew Negri, Australian Institute of Marine Science

Phil Osmond, James Cook University

Ned and Tish Pankhurst, University of Tasmania

Marianne and Lance Pearce, Lizard Island Research Station

Max Rees, Australian Institute of Marine Science

Craig Sambell, The Great Barrier Reef Marine Park Authority

Ulrike Siebeck, University of Queensland

Lyle Vail, Lizard Island Research Station

Cherry Ward, Annandale Christian School

Geoff Ward, James Cook University

Nicole Webster, Australian Institute of Marine Science

Bette Willis, James Cook University

Dirk Zeller, James Cook University

Contents

The Story Behind the Story

THE STORY OF THIS BOOK BEGAN WITH ANOTHER BOOK I WROTE back in 1996. That book was called *Monteverde: Science and Scientists in a Costa Rican Cloud Forest,* and I researched it by traveling to Costa Rica to interview scientists and see how they worked. When *Monteverde* was published in 1997, a lot of people found it interesting—so many, in fact, that my editor at Franklin Watts asked if I'd consider writing a similar book about coral reefs. I thought, "What a terrific idea!"

I've always loved coral reefs and have been fascinated by the abundance, beauty, and diversity of reef animals. Since snorkeling in the Red Sea as a teenager, I've been fortunate enough to scuba dive or snorkel on coral reefs in the Caribbean, Thailand, Tahiti, the Cook Islands, Hawaii, and Australia. When I decided to write a book about coral reefs, however, one of my biggest challenges was choosing a coral reef field research station to visit. After contacting a number of stations over the Internet, I decided that Lizard Island Research Station in Australia was the only place I could meet and interview enough scientists to write a book.

With boundless assistance from LIRS directors Anne Hoggett and Lyle Vail, I began to plan my visit. I decided to go to Lizard Island at the time of the annual coral mass spawning event, and it turns out, this was when many researchers also planned to be there. I e-mailed all of these scientists and asked if they would mind me interviewing them and going out to watch them work. Even though most would be busy running experiments, almost all of them said I'd be welcome.

As I continued to do research on the Web, I learned that the International Tropical Marine Ecosystems Management Symposium was going to be held in Townsville, Australia, about the same time I planned to visit Lizard Island. I decided to fly to Australia a couple of weeks early so I could attend the conference. Listening to biologists and coral reef managers from all over the world, I got a good background on the problems facing the world's coral reefs and what people are doing about them.

Townsville is also the site of James Cook University, so while I was there, I took the opportunity to interview a number of biologists who sometimes worked at Lizard Island, but weren't going to be there during my visit. As an added bonus, I was fortunate enough to get a behind-the-scenes tour of the world's largest coral reef aquarium, Reef HQ (formerly the Great Barrier Reef Aquarium). Biologists there met with me to discuss the challenges of keeping corals in captivity and gave me further insights into the Great Barrier Reef and its ecology.

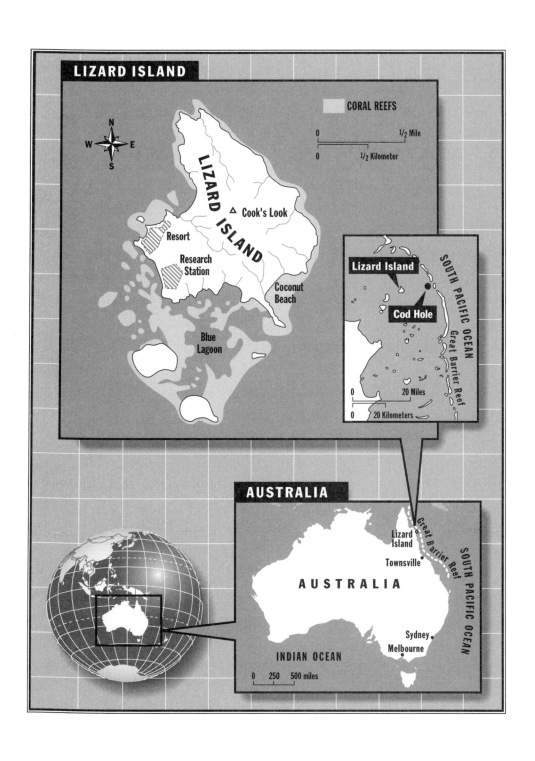

My journey's highlight, of course, was the 2 weeks I actually spent on Lizard Island. Every day I talked to scientists, scuba dived with them, and learned what they were doing. My favorite times were in the evenings, when I had the opportunity listen to stories from Dave Bellwood, Ned Pankhurst, Lexa Grutter, Jeff Leis, Mark McCormick, and other biologists.

The trip wasn't all fun and games. While I was there, I got an ear infection, which made diving painful and kept me from being in the water as much as I wanted. I also ripped open my hand on a piece of coral and had to scrub open the wound twice a day to make sure it didn't get infected. On two dives, my new underwater camera malfunctioned, preventing me from getting several important photographs.

Nonetheless, by the end of my trip I had collected more than 30 hours of interviews, 25 rolls of film, and 100 scientific papers and books. Together, this material—as well as the good humor and warmth of the scientists themselves—made this book possible.

—*Sneed B. Collard III*

ONE

Spawn-a-Thon

"A<small>RE THEY DOING IT YET?</small>" A <small>STUDENT ASKS.</small>

Dr. Andrew Heyward, also known as "Smiley," has already been asked this question a hundred times today. He's been asked by students, by fellow scientists, and by a dozen members of a BBC film crew who are on Lizard Island filming a nature program on coral reefs. Smiley, though, is used to the question. He just flashes his good-natured grin and, in his best Australian accent, replies, "Naw, not yet. I think it's goin' to be tonight, though."

The question on everyone's minds is whether the corals around Lizard Island have begun their annual spawning event, and the only person who can really tell them is Andrew. That's because Andrew is one of the world's leading experts on coral spawning. He is here to gather eggs and sperm for experiments on coral reproduction.

A Jewel in the Crown

Andrew is only one of hundreds of scientists and students who visit Lizard Island each year. Some work on corals. Others work on fish, giant clams, or sea stars. All these people share one purpose: unlocking the many secrets of one of Earth's most spectacular underwater ecosystems—Australia's Great Barrier Reef.

The Great Barrier Reef is not, as its name suggests, a single reef, but a collection of more than 2,800 separate reefs along Australia's eastern coastline. The reefs glitter like living jewels from the Cape York Peninsula all the way south to Brisbane, more than 1,200 miles (2,000 kilometers) away.

The reefs come in many varieties. *Fringing reefs* hug the shorelines of Australia's northern mainland and offshore islands. *Patch reefs* and *coral cays* poke up from shallow offshore waters. Out along the edge of the continental shelf are the most dramatic reefs, the *barrier reefs*. These walls of coral reach down 100 feet (30 meters) below the surface and form a stunning line of defense against the fury of the southern Pacific Ocean.

Visually, the Great Barrier Reef is without question one of the most magnificent places on Earth. However, it is the biology of the Great Barrier Reef that most impresses scientists. More than 2,200 species of fishes, 340 species of corals, and tens of thousands of other *invertebrate* species live along the Great Barrier Reef. Six of the world's seven kinds of sea turtles feed and nest on the reef, as do hundreds of kinds of sea birds. Behind the corals, you'll find manatees and dugongs peacefully grazing on seagrass meadows while, farther out, humpback whales and porpoises frolic in the Coral Sea's opalescent waters.

Lizard Island's First European Visitor

The British explorer Captain James Cook was the first European to set foot on Lizard Island. In 1770, during his first epic round-the-world voyage, Cook became hopelessly trapped within the maze of the Great Barrier Reef. Coral reefs are beautiful to look at, but they can quickly rip a boat to shreds, and several times, Cook almost smashed his ship against the reef's jagged coral "teeth."

After more than 2 months dodging disaster, Cook finally sighted a large island to the east of Cape Flattery. Desperate to escape his coral nightmare, Cook decided to go ashore and climb the island's highest point. From this vantage, now known as Cook's Look, the captain spotted a deep channel through the outer reef and, 2 days later, made his escape back to England. During his stay on the island, however, Cook encountered a number of 4-foot- (1.2-m) long monitor lizards and decided to name the place Lizard Island—a name that has stuck to this day.

Remarkably, our knowledge of the Great Barrier Reef (GBR) has grown very slowly. That is why, in the early 1970s, scientists from the Australian Museum in Sydney considered building a new research station on Lizard Island. At that time, several research stations already operated on the GBR's southern end, but the north remained remote and inaccessible. Australian scientists hoped that a new station would help solve this problem, and in 1973, Lizard Island Research Station, or LIRS, became a reality.

LIRS began modestly, with a couple of temporary buildings, four boats, canvas tents for housing, an air compressor, and fourteen scuba tanks for divers. By 1999, it had grown to include 12 boats, 50 scuba tanks, a state-of-the-art seawater system and aquarium, half a dozen laboratories, and modern accommodations for up to 26 researchers and students at a time. During the past decade, one of the station's regular visitors has been coral biologist Andrew Heyward.

From a modest beginning, Lizard Island Research Station has become one of the most well-equipped marine field stations in the world.

Surf 'n' Spawn

Andrew Heyward grew up in Sydney, Australia's largest city. "My dad worked in banking and my mum was a schoolteacher," Andrew recalls. "They chucked those jobs to start a small cafe at Manly Beach, a famous tourist spot on the north side of Sydney Harbour. I had an idyllic childhood. The family business sat across the road from a great surfing beach. When I wasn't surfing, I went fishing along the shore or in a small dingy. In that part of the world, you learned to surf, handle boats, and understand the sea very, very early in life, so kids were allowed to roam around without much supervision."

Andrew's strong attraction to the ocean sometimes got him in trouble, since he preferred surfing to sitting in class, but it also got him interested in marine biology. After graduating from high school, his love of the sea took him to James Cook University, or JCU, in Townsville, Australia—only a stone's throw away from the Great Barrier Reef.

"I liked James Cook," Andrew recalls. "It was a small, very personal university in those days, and when I moved there from the city, I just got enthusiastic about being in the tropics. It was definitely a sensual delight being in warm tropical places swimming around looking at coral reefs. I'd actually never really thought about coral reefs before, but as I staggered through my first year or two at James Cook, I grew more interested."

After completing his basic undergraduate studies, Andrew went on to do an honors project and then began a graduate Ph.D. program at JCU. His passion was coral reproduction.

The Secret Sex Life of Corals

Corals reproduce in an astounding variety of ways. One of these ways—also shared by many other animals—is *sexual reproduction*, or sex. A sperm from a male coral fertilizes an egg from a female to produce a tiny coral *larva* that eventually grows into an adult coral. Corals, however, face a huge problem not shared by most other animals: they can't move. Once adult corals start growing, they are stuck in place for the rest of their lives. For the eggs and sperm of most corals to find each other, they must be spawned, or released into the water, where they run the risk of getting lost, swept apart, or eaten by fish and other predators.

Corals reproduce in many ways, but spawning allows eggs and sperm from different coral colonies to reach other.

Back in the late 1970s and early 1980s, many scientists asked themselves, "Given all of the hazards coral sperm and eggs face, how do they find each other so consistently?" As Andrew worked on his honors project and applied for graduate school, he, too, became interested in this question.

"We'd been working on coral reproduction at JCU," Andrew recalls, "and in the year after my honors project, the senior graduate students were looking at one or two species of corals and starting to feel that something unusual was going on with their reproduction. This group of graduate students, which I joined, started thinking, 'Maybe these corals are all spawning at the same time.'"

"So when I started graduate school," Andrew continues, "I spent my first summer in Hawaii taking a graduate class on coral population biology. But I also began looking at the Hawaiian corals to see what they were doing reproductively, and I discovered that they spawned. Meanwhile, the team in Townsville discovered that quite a few species were spawning all at once on the Great Barrier Reef. When I came back from Hawaii in 1984, we went all over the reef and found that 105 species spawned in these *mass spawnings*."

Andrew and six other biologists from James Cook University published their findings in the science journal *Marine Biology*. Their discovery totally transformed the way marine scientists thought about coral reproduction and helped chart Andrew's future career.

All Together Now

The Great Barrier Reef's coral mass spawning event is truly one of Earth's most amazing spectacles. Around Lizard Island, the spawning occurs a few nights after the last full moon in spring, usually between mid-November and mid-December. The timing varies in different parts of the Great Barrier Reef, but coincides with rising sea temperatures, the phase of the moon, and moderate tides. More than 135 species of corals can participate in the event. During heavy spawnings, the corals cover the sea surface with huge slicks containing trillions of sperm and pink and white eggs.

Mass spawnings also occur on other reefs. Several species may spawn together in the Red Sea and the Carribean, for example, but far fewer species take part than on the Great Barrier Reef and reefs nearby.

Mass spawning offers many advantages to the Great Barrier Reef's corals. By releasing all their eggs at once, corals overwhelm predators that feed on the eggs. Fish and other egg-eaters quickly stuff themselves on this feast, but leave the rest of the eggs to go on their merry way.

The spawning also helps different coral colonies *cross-fertilize*. Many kinds of corals have both male and female reproductive organs, and a lot of these corals can fertilize their own eggs. Having an egg fertilized by a sperm from a different coral colony, however, can prevent inbreeding and lead to healthier larvae. It can also create new genetic combinations, which lead to improved varieties of corals. If the corals didn't spawn at the same time, sperm and eggs from different colonies would never reach each other and cross-fertilization would be impossible.

A third advantage is that mass spawning allows corals of more than one species to *hybridize*. In land animals, two different species can rarely mate with each other successfully, but apparently this is not true of corals. Bette Willis, one of Andrew Heyward's colleagues, examined forty-two different coral species and found that one-third of them readily hybridize with other species. Again, this may help corals succeed, since new genetic combinations of corals may be better able to survive than older ones.

Eggs Galore

Although the discovery of the mass coral spawning event answered some questions about coral reproduction, it raised a lot of others, especially for Andrew. He, in fact, is not as interested in the actual spawning event as much as in using it to investigate other mysteries about coral reproduction. He tackles these mysteries by going to a reef where a spawning event is about to take place. When the corals spawn, he collects a large number of eggs and sperm. Then, he conducts experiments on the eggs and on the larvae that develop.

During spawning, Andrew Heyward brings corals into tanks and aquariums. As they spawn, he uses a simple suction device to collect their eggs and sperm for his experiments.

If Andrew's experiments don't work out during one spawning, he simply goes to another one a month or two later. Over the years, he and other scientists have determined where and when coral spawning takes place in almost every region of the world. One month, he may be working in Australia, another month in Hawaii, the Philippines, or southern Japan.

Recently, Andrew has tried to answer several specific questions at Lizard Island. One has to do with what causes coral larvae to settle. Like many ocean animals, corals go through a *larval stage* before they become adults. After the corals release their sperm and eggs, fertilization takes place and the fertilized eggs grow into tiny free-floating larvae. Currents carry the larvae to many places on the reef, but at some point—usually after about a week—the larvae settle to the bottom and begin growing into adult corals.

One big question Andrew and other biologists have is: How do the larvae know *where* to settle? If they picked spots at random, most of them would surely die. Many would settle on sand, which would smother them. Others would settle in places that are too deep or too shallow for them to survive. What's amazing, though, is that many of the larvae settle in the right places—places where other corals are growing successfully or can grow successfully. How do they do it?

Andrew and other researchers are pretty sure that larvae can "taste" chemicals in the ocean. These chemicals may be released from adult corals or, more likely, from algae that are growing on the reef. To find out exactly what the larvae are keying in on, Andrew and his team conduct a variety of experiments. In one, they place small terra-cotta tiles out on the reef. They cover half of each tile with nylon mesh, like panty hose, and leave the other half exposed. They leave these tiles on the reef for more than 2 months to allow bacteria, flat *crustose algae*, and other small organisms to grow on the exposed halves of the tiles.

After the spawning event, Andrew's team dives down to the terra-cotta tiles and removes the nylon from the covered half of each tile. This leaves one half of each tile entirely clean and the other half covered with algae and other organisms that have grown on it. Then, they pump coral larvae from special holding pools down to where the tiles are. Over the next few days, Andrew and his team closely observe which tiles—and which parts of the tiles—the larvae choose to settle on. Do they settle on the clean halves of the tiles? The "dirty" halves? Do they settle near the crustose algae? On top of bacteria?

Larval Landings

From these experiments, Andrew has found that, given a chance, coral larvae settle near flat, crustose algae that are growing on the tiles he places underwater. However, he's also found that currents, light, and other factors can easily prevent the larvae from settling in the best locations. These results are interesting by themselves, but they also can help us learn more about reef regeneration. After a cyclone or other disaster damages a reef, some reefs recover better than others. Why? Andrew's studies suggest that perhaps it is because some reefs have the right algae to attract new coral larvae and others don't. Or it could be because other factors are interfering with coral settlement.

"If a reef is degraded by human activities," Andrew explains, "like pollution or runoff, and someone's trying to figure out how to respond, usually the person will say 'Well, if just a one-time event like a cyclone or oil spill hurt the reef, it will probably recover naturally as long as new coral larvae reach the reef each year.' But when there are chronic stresses on the reef, year after year, it's hard to tell whether it will recover naturally or not.

"So putting these little tiles into damaged habitats can be a real tool. If the young corals survive on the tiles, you know that conditions are probably adequate for the reef to recover. However, if the young corals don't survive, there's obviously still some condition that is killing them and needs to be fixed before the reef can recover."

Toxic Techniques

Andrew has many other coral questions he's trying to answer. One is how different pollutants might interfere with coral reproduction. While Andrew busily gathers eggs on Lizard Island, his colleague Andrew Negri runs *toxicology* experiments. In these experiments, he exposes coral eggs and sperm to different human-made pollutants to see if they interfere with fertilization and larval settlement. The pollutants include copper and tin, which are ingredients in *antifouling compounds*—compounds that are painted on ships' hulls to keep organisms from growing on them. The pollutants also include raw petroleum, which might come from an oil spill, as well as the chemicals people spray on oil spills to break them up.

"We're finding that if you compare copper and tin," explains Andrew, "copper is much more toxic to fertilization, but tin is much more toxic to the larvae during settlement. So that debunks the idea that the younger the corals are, the more vulnerable they are. They *are* vulnerable, but we need to understand exactly when and why certain compounds are harmful. We can't presume that corals are more sensitive just because they are in a particular life stage."

Andrew's team has also discovered that at least one of the chemicals people use to break up oil spills is more harmful to larvae than the oil itself. These and other results will help managers decide what chemicals can be safely introduced to the water surrounding coral reefs and how people should respond to oil spills and other chemical disasters.

Andrew Negri exposes eggs and sperm to different pollutants to see whether they interfere with coral fertilization.

CORAL REEF BRIEF

Earth's Incredible Corals

Like sea jellies and sea anemones, scientists classify corals as *Cnidaria*. Corals can be found in a variety of ocean habitats, including warm tropical waters, polar seas, and along the floor of the deep sea. Not all corals build reefs. Many corals—especially in cooler, temperate waters—live as individuals or as part of a small colony. However, reef-building corals have special qualities that many other corals don't possess.

Reef-building corals, such as this staghorn coral (below), live in large colonies that may consist of thousands of individual polyps (right).

All reef-building corals are made up of many units called *polyps* that live together. Each individual polyp has its own tentacles, mouth, stomach, and often, sex organs. But each polyp is also connected to other polyps to form a kind of "superanimal" called a *colony*. When you see a large brain coral or a branching staghorn, you are actually looking at thousands of individual polyps all growing together in a colony.

Reef-building corals live only in clear, sunlit waters. One reason is because reef-building corals have microscopic single-celled *zooxanthellae* living inside of them. These tiny organisms find shelter within a coral's body, but they also use the sun's energy and the coral's waste products to make food. Reef-building corals need plenty of sunlight to survive because, although corals catch small prey with their stinger-filled tentacles, a large portion of their food comes from zooxanthellae.

One final difference between reef-building corals and other corals is that all reef-building

Symbiotic zooxanthellae can be seen as gray areas in this close-up of coral polyps.

corals live in warm waters. No one is sure why, but one theory involves calcium. A reef's structure comes from the hard *calcium carbonate* skeletons that the corals secrete. Some scientists believe that calcium is easier to extract from warm water than cold water, and that explains why coral reefs only develop in the warm tropics.

Scientists are especially fascinated by coral reproduction and genetics. Most corals reproduce sexually. Many spawn, or release their eggs and sperm into the water. In others, fertilization takes place inside the corals' bodies, and the larvae are *brooded* until they are more mature and have a better chance of surviving the reef's many predators.

Corals also reproduce *asexually*, without fertilization. Some produce larvae without sex. Many others produce buds or other structures that separate from a colony to grow into new "daughter" colonies. Pieces of some large colonies—especially those of fragile, branching corals such as staghorn corals—*fragment*, or break off, to grow into new colonies.

Corals have many other unusual features as well. Scientists think that some coral colonies can actually fuse together to create new, larger colonies. Other colonies may be able to mutate. In some cases, one part of a colony may mutate into a slightly different form while another part of the colony stays the same. During spawning, different species of corals sometimes hybridize to form brand-new species or types.

All of this can drive a geneticist crazy. With many land animals, a biologist can easily work out the relationships between individuals and species by looking at their DNA. Not with corals. The genetics of corals are so complicated that it's often impossible to tell which corals are related to others or even whether two colonies are the same or different species!

Researchers will spend many more years unraveling the complex world of coral biology. However, scientists already appreciate that the "craziness" of corals may give the animals huge advantages. Early naturalists looked at coral reefs as stable, peaceful places, but researchers now know that the exact opposite is true. Cyclones often tear apart reefs. Sea stars devour others. Disease can hammer an entire reef or species, while unusually warm water temperatures or intense sunlight can kill most corals at a given place and time.

With so many uncertainties, the species of corals alive today, may be the ones that have had the widest array of options for reproducing and surviving. These survivors may also have the best chances of coping with the challenges we humans throw at them now and in the future.

Two

Running a Research Station

ANNE HOGGETT SWIMS IN A METHODICAL, ZIGZAG PATTERN just above a patch reef. Her eyes dart back and forth, scanning every branch in the thicket of blue and white staghorn corals beneath her. Once in a while, she pauses to study a spot more closely, but then she moves on, breathing through her scuba gear at a slow, steady pace. As she swims in toward the reef's center, she suddenly stops and takes an extra gulp of air through her regulator. She pulls out a 20-inch- (50-centimeter) long needle attached to a large squirt bottle and reaches down toward her prey—a cleverly concealed crown-of-thorns sea star, or COTS.

The COTS has been happily munching away on the living coral and has already done quite a bit of damage. Its arms stretch more than 12 inches (30 cm) across and bristle with hard, sharp spines that make the sea star virtually impossible for other animals to eat. Anne doesn't want to eat the COTS, however. She wants to keep it from eating any more coral. Inserting the long needle just beneath the skin of the sea star, she injects a solution of sodium bisulfate, a chemical that will kill her prey without harming any other reef creatures. Satisfied that she has removed one more thorny menace from the reef, Anne kicks her swim fins and continues her sea star search.

Lizard Island Research Station

Keeping up with COTS is just one of many duties Anne shares with her husband and fellow biologist, Lyle Vail. Since 1990, Anne and Lyle have served as the directors of the Lizard Island Research Station. As directors, they are responsible for long-term plans to improve LIRS and make it a better place for scientists to work. They also handle hundreds of details that keep the station functioning from day to day. When they began their careers, however, neither of them expected they would one day be living and working in one of the world's most beautiful locations.

"I grew up in Minnesota," Lyle explains. "I earned a bachelor's degree from St. Olaf's, a small private school that had a connection with a marine lab in the Florida Keys. I went there a couple of times and got really interested in the ocean. After graduating, I went into the Peace Corps and lived in Thailand for 2 years. Then, instead of going back to the United States, I went to Australia and earned a master's degree. After that, I got a job at Sydney University and began working at the Australian Museum."

In contrast to Lyle, Anne is a native "Aussie" who, like Andrew Heyward, spent her youth in Sydney. "I grew up on the water in Sydney Harbor and spent a lot of time sailing and boating," she says. "I learned to dive when I was 15 years old and have been snorkeling ever since I can remember. Ever since I was about 12, I have known exactly what I wanted to do—become a marine biologist."

Anne pursued her interest in marine science at the University of New South Wales. Afterward, she began working at the Australian Museum and, 5 years later, started working on her Ph.D. While working at the museum, Anne met Lyle. The two married and had their son, Alex. While they worked on their Ph.D.s, Anne and Lyle also conducted research on Lizard Island. "I suppose that's when we fell in love with the place," Lyle explains.

Anne and Lyle decided that one day, they'd like to run LIRS, but they had no idea how or when. Then, they spotted the break they'd been looking for.

"It was really quite odd," Anne recalls. "We had contacted the Australian Museum to let them know we were interested in the job and to let us know if it became available. When it came up, though, many people at the museum weren't even aware the job was being advertised. We were eating breakfast at somebody's place up in Darwin and reading the weekend newspaper when somebody said, 'Oh, here's a good job.' It turned out, it was the directors' job at LIRS."

Big Ideas, Little Details

When they assumed the helm of LIRS, Anne and Lyle wanted to accomplish many things. "We've got a 15-year plan that we drew up 6 or 7 years ago," Anne explains. "When we drew it up, we thought, 'Aw yeah, this is all pie in the sky. If we get half that, we'll be doing well.' But actually, we're right on target, and nobody's more surprised than we are."

With persistence, creative financing, and support from the Australian Museum and private donors, Anne and Lyle have been able to build new laboratories at LIRS, improve living conditions for scientists, install a new seawater system for keeping live animals, and buy new generators to provide LIRS with electricity.

It's the daily tasks of running the station that keep the two directors busiest, however. With up to thirty scientists and students living and working at the station at any one time, Anne and Lyle are confronted with an endless array of problems and challenges. These range from getting medicine for scientists who fall ill to taking reservations for researchers who want to visit to advising biologists on where they can find the animals or ecosystems they want to work with.

As directors, Anne and Lyle also must inform the public and the Australian Museum about what they're doing, host student groups who

A rare glimpse of LIRS directors Anne Hoggett and Lyle Vail in their office. Most of the time, running LIRS keep them on the move.

come to experience the Great Barrier Reef firsthand, write reports to the station's fund-raising foundation, speak at fund-raising dinners, respond to questions from reporters, and help develop long-term management plans for the reef.

And then there are the emergencies. "There's always a few major dramas each year," Lyle explains. "A big problem, for example, is when the pump for the aquarium breaks. We've got experiments going on almost all the time in aquariums. If the pump stops for more than a few hours, we're in trouble because we'll lose all the animals we've got. Of course, things like that always seem to happen in the middle of the night," Lyle says with a laugh.

"Sometimes one of the scientists has a medical emergency early in the morning," Anne adds. "But helping them out is just part of our job. Most people are pretty considerate. They don't disturb us unless they really need to."

Still, Anne and Lyle never know when something unexpected will crop up. Not long ago, for instance, two people who were volunteering at LIRS decided to take a walk to one of the island's most breathtaking spots, Coconut Beach. This wide beach of brilliant white sand lies at the back of a cove. It's a popular destination for hikers and boaters, but it's also a place where people can get into trouble.

"Coconut Beach has a very wide, shallow *reef flat* in front of it," Anne explains. "And it is bounded on both ends by steep granite slopes. During most of the year, strong onshore winds make it inaccessible by boat. To get there, you have to walk or take a boat to Lizard Head, then climb over Lizard Head and walk in through the shallows on the reef flat. The only alternative is to scale the steep granite cliff at the end of the beach, but most people find that quite difficult."

"Anyway," Anne continues, "the volunteers went to Coconut Beach during a very low tide and stayed too long. When they wanted to get back to Lizard Head, they encountered rolling waves up to their waists, and the tide was surging in. One of the volunteers couldn't swim and was not willing to tackle the 500-yard [450 m] walk against surf and a rising tide. Unfortunately, there was no other way out.

"Luckily, an agile camper was also on the beach. He was able to climb the granite cliff and run the couple of miles to the research station for help. Lyle and I went to the top of the cliff and shouted down to the volunteers that we couldn't get a boat in to rescue them because it was too dangerous. We told them they'd have to wait for the tide to drop—at 2:30 A.M. the following morning! With no other options, we returned to Lizard Head in the early hours with flashlights and walked in through the shallows to guide the tired and cold volunteers back to the Station."

Anne admits this was a harrowing experience for the volunteers and the rescuers. "But," she adds with a good-natured grin, "one benefit of this midnight adventure was that we got to see a lot of sleeping sea turtles on the reef flat."

Time for Research

Anne and Lyle's experience and clearheadedness allow them to meet most challenges that arise at LIRS. Their dedication and knowledge of the reef, however, also let them help hundreds of scientists make the most of their time at LIRS each year. Part of what makes the duo so valuable is that they are biologists themselves and are familiar with the needs of the researchers who come to Lizard Island.

As busy as they are, however, Anne and Lyle still find time to con-duct a bit of research themselves. One of their projects has to do with a place called the Cod Hole. In the 1970s, two famous biologists and photographers, Valerie and Ron Taylor, discovered a place near the outer barrier reef that seemed to be a gathering place for giant fish known as potato cod.

Growing up to 6.5 feet (2 m) long and weighing 200 pounds (91 kilograms), potato cod are members of the grouper family. They are prized for their delicious taste and have been vigorously pursued by people fishing for sport. Before the discovery of the Cod Hole, divers

The Cod Hole provides divers with a rare opportunity to come face-to-face with giant potato cod. Unfortunately, cod numbers have decreased as the spot's popularity has risen.

had observed the fish only alone or in pairs. As word of the Cod Hole got out, divers swarmed to the site. They wanted to see and feed these gigantic fish, and soon the Cod Hole became a regular stop for dive boats from all over the northern Great Barrier Reef.

Unfortunately, as the number of tourists visiting the Cod Hole increased, the number of cod began to decrease. Anne and Lyle wondered what was going on. They began working with the dive boat operator from the nearby Lizard Island Resort to count the numbers of potato cod each time the boat went out. Since 1992, they've asked diving guides from the resort to fill out questionnaires that might reveal something about the cod.

"During the first year of the study," Lyle explains, "the *mean* number of fish observed at the site at any one time was somewhere around twelve, with a maximum of twenty-six fish. As time went by, the mean number of fish dropped off significantly. Now, we generally see around seven fish at a time, and the most we ever see is twelve."

Anne and Lyle aren't sure what has caused the decline. One possibility is that fish may be injuring each other as they try to get food from the divers. "But the fluctuation in numbers might be a normal variation or it might be due to human activities at the Cod Hole or nearby," says Anne. "To learn more, we've suggested to the Great Barrier Reef Marine Park Authority that they should fund a study to see where the cod go when they aren't at the Cod Hole."

Crown-of-Thorns Sea Stars

Perhaps Anne and Lyle's most interesting research involves the crown-of-thorns sea star, or COTS, an animal that has played a huge role in the history of the Great Barrier Reef.

The modern history of COTS began in the early 1960s. At the time, tourists were just beginning to visit the Great Barrier Reef to swim, relax, and pursue a brand-new sport known as scuba diving. In 1962, some scuba divers made a shocking discovery near Cairns in northern Queensland: the Great Barrier Reef was being eaten! Suddenly, from out of nowhere, millions of large, spiny crown-of-thorns sea stars were swarming over the coral, devouring everything in sight and turning miles of reefs into rubble. A cry of alarm swept through the scientific world. Many researchers predicted that the spine-covered invaders would devastate, perhaps even destroy, the Great Barrier Reef.

They didn't.

Today, after almost 40 years, two more COTS outbreaks, and intensive scientific study, biologists have come to believe that COTS are a part of the reef's natural cycle. The outbreaks seem to occur every 15

The crown-of-thorns sea star is one of the few animals that eats living corals. It is the subject of intensive scientific study.

to 17 years. Scientists believe that an abundance of food triggers the COTS population explosions. A mature female COTS can produce more than 60 million eggs in a year. If there is plenty of microscopic algae in the water for the COTS larvae to eat, and plenty of hard corals for the adult COTS to feed on, populations can increase very quickly— and with dramatic results.

During the 1970s and 1980s, COTS attacked almost one-fifth of the 2,800 reefs that make up the Great Barrier Reef. Five percent of the GBR's reefs were severely damaged. COTS outbreaks have also occurred in the Indian Ocean, along the coasts of Asia, and in the South Pacific. The most recent Great Barrier Reef outbreak began in 1994 near Lizard Island.

COTS Control

"We were expecting the next COTS outbreak," recalls Anne, "and we thought if it's going to start somewhere, it's going to start here, so we were watching for it. But when we finally noticed the numbers starting to increase, it took us by surprise how quickly it became a problem. One minute, the COTS weren't very common; 6 months later, we had a full invasion."

Although Anne and Lyle recognized that COTS were a natural phenomenon, they also saw value in protecting some of Lizard Island's reefs. They wanted to figure out how best to control the COTS at reefs that were popular with divers and other tourists. Working under a contract from the CRC Reef Research Centre in Townsville, Anne and Lyle selected six reefs near Lizard Island and experimented with different approaches to killing the COTS by injecting them with sodium bisulfate. "The study showed that the best way of protecting the reefs was to kill all the COTS fairly frequently—going back there time and time again and killing every COTS we found," Anne explains.

Besides learning how to control COTS on a small scale, the study had an additional benefit. While most of Lizard Island's reefs were "eaten out" by the recent invasion, Anne and Lyle were able to keep two of the reefs clear of COTS and protect their corals. These reefs provide a valuable reference for scientists visiting Lizard Island because they can examine the differences between healthy and damaged reefs and the animals that live there.

Life After COTS

The COTS themselves continue to be a source of interest and concern for scientists. While most biologists believe that COTS population explosions are natural, many think that human activities may be increasing their frequency. For example, coastal runoff from farms may increase nutrient levels in the ocean and provide more food for COTS larvae.

To learn more about COTS, the Australian Institute of Marine Science, the Great Barrier Reef Marine Park Authority, and other scientific groups have carried out extensive monitoring and research on COTS. This work, in turn, has led to research on many other aspects of the Great Barrier Reef.

As the latest COTS invasion subsides around Lizard Island, the reefs that did get eaten are beginning to recover. Fast-growing staghorn and table corals are once again sprouting up, offering fresh opportunities for research and repeating a cycle that may be as old as the Great Barrier Reef itself. For Anne and Lyle, these cycles add a richness to their work on Lizard Island—work they realize is unique.

"It's amazing to be able to take a swim out in the front yard and swim over a reef," Lyle reflects. "We spend a lot of time just on management and fund-raising, but I think our ultimate goal is to get high-quality research done on the reef and that certainly is happening. It wouldn't happen if we didn't have a good facility."

"Also," Lyle continues, "it's important to have a place where educational groups can come and experience the reef. A lot of students come through here. This is where they learn about fieldwork, how to use a boat, and how to do things underwater. This is a training area. If scientists didn't have places like this, the only alternative would be to go out on a big research vessel, and that's much more expensive. In the end, a lot of young, up-and-coming scientists probably wouldn't get trained in a proper manner. Ultimately, the reefs would suffer."

THREE

The Fish Mechanic

As THE 23-FOOT (7-M) BOAT ROUNDS THE WINDWARD SIDE OF Palfrey Island, a powerful squall slams into it. Thirty-mile- (50-km) - per-hour gusts drive rain sideways into the bow, dropping visibility to a couple hundred yards and obscuring landmarks in every direction. Within moments, waves rise from 4 inches to 5 feet (10 cm to 1.5 m) high, smacking the boat's hull and knocking the craft up and down like a bathtub toy. Through it all, fish biologist David Bellwood keeps his good humor.

"Bit breezy today," he comments wryly in his northern English accent. "What do you think Phil?"

Phil Osmond, David's dive officer, guides the boat through the waves as if he is driving a minivan to the corner grocery store to buy milk. Steering by compass into the teeth of the squall, he looks at the rain and waves and mutters, "Aw, I think it'll pass."

Minutes later, the storm worsens. The waves grow bigger. The rain falls harder. Visibility drops to almost zero. After another hundred jarring waves and more consultation with Phil, David decides they'd better abandon their original destination—a patch reef about 5 miles (8 km) away—and spend the day in the calm of Lizard Island's Blue Lagoon. Far from being disappointed, however, David exudes irrepressible good cheer. Squall or not, he is experiencing his best field expedition in years, and he is about to spend the day with his favorite underwater companions: tropical reef fish.

Colors—Who Needs 'Em?

When most people visit a coral reef, the first things they notice are the fish. Divers and snorkelers ooh and aah over the shapes, sizes, and more than anything, the spectacular colors of reef fish. David Bellwood couldn't care less about a fish's colors. He's interested in how a fish works and what it's like inside. He credits a lot of that interest to his father.

David grew up in a working-class family in Huddersfield, an industrial city in Yorkshire, England, where his father worked as a plumber and electrician. As a youth, David often worked alongside his dad, serving as an apprentice after school and during summer holidays. His father showed him how to maintain heating systems and how various textile mill machines operate. "Whenever something broke down," David recalls, "he taught me how to take it apart and fix it. One of the most important parts of doing this was making sure I knew how to put it back together again."

When David wasn't going to school or helping his dad, tropical fish swam through his head. "The beginning of my interest in marine biology, I suppose, was keeping live fish," David remarks. "When I was 11 years old, I started keeping coral reef fish in aquariums. Back in those days, tropical fish usually died. People told me, 'Don't try it son, there's no way you'll succeed,' but that was wonderful because the more they said that, the more I wanted to try it."

"One of the main reasons the fish usually didn't survive is because the people who collected them in the wild used cyanide to stun and capture them," David continues. "Of course, at the time, no one knew that cyanide harmed the fish. But I was curious. I wanted to find out how cyanide affected the fish. I wondered if I could demonstrate how the cyanide acted in their bodies. Basically, that started my interest in biology."

David pursued his interest by studying animal physiology at the University of Bath in southwest England. After graduating with honors, he decided to plunge into the world's largest coral reef aquarium—the Great Barrier Reef.

Lever Heads

In 1981, David moved to Townsville, Australia, to begin his postgraduate studies at James Cook University. When he began his Ph.D., he wasn't sure exactly what he wanted to do, but he knew it had to have something to do with fish. "At first," he explains, "I thought I'd work on lionfish behavior and ecology, but lionfish are rare on the Great Barrier Reef, and I couldn't find any. So then I chose parrotfishes because they are common and little was known about them."

For his Ph.D. research, David began looking at the feeding biology of parrotfishes, especially how their heads and jaws work. Again, he drew inspiration from his father. "The heads of fishes use the same

The Biological Sciences building at James Cook University houses the offices of David Bellwood and many more of the world's leading coral reef biologists.

principles my father had taught me," he explains. "If you look at the jaws of a parrotfish, for example, you can see that they are compound levers and you can predict how they will move. If you see a muscle, you know what it can do and why the angle of the muscle fibers will give you a certain amount of strength and force. All in all, fish heads are a lot like the machines I grew up with."

After finishing his Ph.D., David wanted to put his knowledge to practical use. "I was really keen on conservation," he explains. "I did all kinds of work. I worked on fisheries to understand how we exploit the fish. I worked on conservation programs in the Philippines for a year. I was very keen to stop the cyanide trade there or at least find out whether it was as harmful as we thought."

Unfortunately, David's work in the Philippines showed him that conservation alone couldn't save the coral reefs there. He recognized that the main problem in the Philippines, and many other developing countries, is overpopulation. As long as millions of desperately poor people are trying to make a living along the coasts, the reefs and the animals that live on them stand little chance of surviving. With this sad realization, David decided to return to work on the Great Barrier Reef—a place that does stand a chance because of Australia's relatively small population.

Fish Machines

After returning to Australia, David began working with Howard Choat at James Cook University. He decided to pick up where he had left off—with parrotfishes. "Even though, I had started studying parrotfishes almost by accident," David explains, "once I actually started working on them, I began to realize how important they are in the reef system."

David set out to learn all he could about parrotfishes. He wanted to understand the roles different parrotfishes play on the Great Barrier Reef. "A fish," he explains, "only interacts with the reef in two places—its mouth and its anus. Those are the contact points. I was interested in what a fish has in its mouth and what comes out of the hole in its back end. I knew that focusing on how each kind of parrotfish bites was the key to understanding the interaction between the reef and the fish.

"Take two parrotfishes, for example. They look the same, with similar body shapes and bright, lovely colors, and they both feed on coral. They seem to be doing the same thing, but if you peel away their skins, you find that they're completely different inside. One has massive teeth and bites big chunks of dead coral out of the reef. The other has thinner, lighter teeth and is busy scraping the reef surface."

To learn more about parrotfish-reef interactions, David began a study following two species of parrotfishes. He began diving at different

David Bellwood has studied fish on many of the world's coral reefs. Here, at age 21, he captures a fish in the Red Sea.

places around Lizard Island every day, watching every single thing members of the two species did. He followed the fish around and recorded how many bites they were taking and where they were taking them. He measured how big the bites were and what they looked like. He even recorded how often the fish defecated and tried to measure the amount of waste material. According to David, "They don't defecate where they're eating. They usually do it several meters away, and where one goes, they all go. It's like this bombing raid. At these toilet sites, you often find piles and piles of sediments."

Fish Versus Fishes

For nonscientists, the word "fish" means either one fish or, as a plural, more than one fish. Scientists, however, also use the word "fishes." When a scientist uses the word "fishes," she or he is referring to more than one fish species.

For scientists—and nonscientists—a big school of tuna, for example, would be a school of fish. However, a group of fish that consists of a potato cod, a coral trout, a butterfly fish, a triggerfish, and a surgeonfish would be a school of fishes. So when scientists talk about "the biology of reef fishes," they are referring to the biology of the different fish species that live on the coral reef—not just a random school of coral reef fish.

Parrotfish Surprise

David's hours of underwater observations led him to a startling discovery: the two species of parrotfishes he was studying had a huge impact on the reef. A single parrotfish of one species removed more than a *ton* of dead coral from the reef each year, turning it into sand. An individual of the second species ate far less, but still removed about 58 pounds (26 kg) of dead coral each year.

When David multiplied the number of parrotfish on the reef by the amount of coral each was removing, the results were astonishing. On some reefs, the amount of dead coral the parrotfish ate equaled the amount of new coral growth each year. The parrotfishes' voracious feeding was actually shaping the topography of the reefs in many places. "They basically removed all the bumps," David explains.

David was so fascinated by his findings that he began looking at other major families of coral reef fish. "My main goal is to identify fish groups that have a major impact on the reef," he says. "Every year when I teach a course in reef fish biology, I give my students a research project. I assign each of them a fish group and say, 'O.K., let's say a foreign company wants to pay the Australian government $1 million for fishing rights to just that group of fish. For that price, the company can fish as much as it wants and can even destroy the fish group completely, but they won't harm the environment in any other way.' The student's job is to find out as much as possible about his or her fish group to see if removing it will harm the reef. Should the company be allowed to take the fish?

"Most of my students answer 'No.' But what strikes me the most is that no one can find enough information on these different fish groups to really answer the question. If someone comes to me and says, 'I want to remove all the parrotfishes,' I can explain how that will harm the reef. But if someone asks, 'What's the effect of removing half of the damselfishes?' my answer is, 'I don't know! We've only just figured out what damselfishes are eating.' There are these huge question marks. What I'm trying to do is, first of all, accept that we know almost nothing and, second, try to determine the kinds of information we need to answer the big questions about these different fish groups."

Fish Food

In addition to parrotfishes, David and his graduate students have taken a close look at surgeonfishes and are studying the reef's largest fish family, the labrids, or wrasses. The work involves monitoring what and how each fish species eats and dissecting each one to understand its anatomy. In fact, David and his colleague Howard Choat have spent the last decade opening up fish and examining their mouthparts, stomachs, and intestines. Their findings have challenged many old beliefs about the role of various fishes on the reef.

"Most of the fish that we think of as herbivores—those that eat large algae—probably aren't," David explains. "When we look at these so-called herbivores, we find that some don't eat any algae at all. Others eat algae, but only a little bit of their energy comes from it. The rest of their energy probably comes from the bacteria and *detritus* they ingest."

By understanding what fish really eat, David is moving closer to his overall goal of understanding the roles of different fishes on the reef and which ones are most important.

"On the Great Barrier Reef," he says, "there are more than 2,200 species of fish, and in the Red Sea there are only 250. Yet the Red Sea

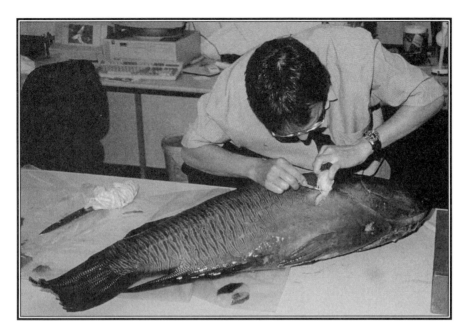

David Bellwood dissects fish, such as this large Napoleon wrasse, to learn more about their mouthparts, stomachs, and intestines.

has coral reefs that function perfectly well. So the question is, could we get rid of 1,950 species of Great Barrier Reef fishes and still have a viable reef? The answer is probably 'Yes,' but only if we remove the right ones. So then you ask, 'But what are the right ones?' To answer that, we need to learn some basic information. That's what we've been trying to do."

The Big Bites

Now an associate professor at James Cook University, David still has a long way to go in understanding how fish influence the reef, but he and his colleagues have begun to put some of the big pieces in place. "The main thing we need to keep the coral reef system working," David suggests, "is *herbivory*. We need animals to remove large algae. Whether fish digest the algae or not doesn't matter, but it appears that they must remove it."

The theory is that removing algae—big algae—is important because if it is not removed, it will rob corals of light and prevent them from growing. That's because the zooxanthellae living inside the corals need light to make the food that reef-building corals need to survive. If large algae covered the corals, the zooxanthellae wouldn't receive enough sunlight and the corals would starve.

A second big piece of the fish-reef puzzle has to do with predators. "Circumstantial evidence," David explains, "suggests that we could remove the big predator fish, such as coral trout and mackerel, without doing a lot of damage to the system. This is good news because coral trout and mackerel are some of the most popular game fish on the reef. If removing them damaged the coral reef system, then the Great Barrier Reef could be in big trouble."

Fish Fossils

When David isn't out in the field, he spends a great deal of time studying fish fossils in an attempt to understand how today's coral reef fish evolved and how the Great Barrier Reef differs from ancient reefs. One thing he's learned is that evolution doesn't travel in a straight line. By studying fish fossils from an ancient coral reef bed in Monte Bolca, Italy, David discovered that most of the groups of reef fish we find in the world today existed 50 million years ago. However, some of the fish groups in the ancient reef bed have now totally disappeared.

"People think that everything evolves toward bigger and better animals," David says, "but that's not always true. At Monte Bolca, there were more fish families than we have today. For instance, there were twice as many groups of surgeonfishes at Bolca as there are today. Today's coral reef fish aren't necessarily better than their ancestors. They may just be the lucky survivors of catastrophic events that drove other fish groups extinct."

In his quest to understand where today's coral reef fishes came from, David is now examining fossils that are even older than the ones from Monte Bolca. Together with his research at Lizard Island, these investigations are helping scientists understand the vital roles and importance of today's coral reef fish—and that their beauty and value are much more than skin-deep.

This fossilized surgeonfish lived more than 50 million years ago. It is one of the many Monte Bolca fossils that David Bellwood has studied to learn about the evolution of coral reef fish.

CORAL REEF BRIEF

Fish Father

When you talk to fish biologists working on the Great Barrier Reef, the name of one man comes up again and again: Howard Choat.

"He's modest about it," says David Bellwood. "But he's had a major impact on the scientists who work here. In many ways, he was the founding father of good marine biology in Australia."

Born in Wellington, New Zealand, Howard fell in love with fish the first time he put on a mask and snorkel as a teenager. Ever since, he has passionately pursued a career in marine science. He earned his undergraduate and master's degrees at Victoria University in Wellington and his Ph.D. at the University of Queensland in Brisbane. In 1971, he landed an academic position at Auckland University where he began building a dynasty of students, graduate students, and postdoctoral students all looking at fish. Then, in 1986, he moved to James Cook University and created a new dynasty of biologists working on the Great Barrier Reef.

Howard began his career looking at *gender-changing* fishes such as parrotfishes. Back then, researchers recognized that some fishes change gender during their lives, but Howard was one of the first people to investigate and describe how widespread this phenomenon is. Since then, Howard has pursued an incredible variety of fish-related interests, either directly or through a legion of students and colleagues including David Bellwood, Mark McCormick, and Brigid Kerrigan.

Age that Fish

"My current research interests are twofold," Howard explains. "They concern firstly the biology of reef fishes with an emphasis on age and age-associated properties. I am also studying herbivorous, or plant-eating, fishes. I'm trying to find out whether the so-called herbivores are truly eating large algae."

For many years, biologists believed that determining a coral reef fish's age was pretty simple. They thought that fish keep growing until they die. Therefore, all small fish must be fairly young, and all large fish must be much older. If the members of a species never seemed to get large, scientists reasoned that they must have short life spans. On the other hand, if they saw large individuals of a particular species, they believed that the species had a longer life span.

Howard Choat turned these "fishy" ideas upside down. As he examined the ear bones, or *otoliths*, of fishes, he discovered that a fish adds a new ring to its otolith every day—much like a tree adds a growth ring every year. By studying a fish's otolith, he could determine its age precisely.

When he examined various Great Barrier Reef fishes, Howard found that many of the smaller fishes, such as surgeonfishes and butterflyfishes, were quite old. Similarly, many of the larger fishes, such as parrotfishes and the giant Maori wrasse, were relatively young and short-lived. In the process, Howard made a startling discovery—many fishes do not keep growing their entire lives. Instead, they grow to their full size very quickly and then live another 40 or 50 years, just like humans do.

Howard Choat's work has shown that many smaller species, such as this butterflyfish (right), are some of the longest-lived. Large wrasses (left), on the other hand, are relatively short lived.

Fish Guts

Like his former postdoctoral student David Bellwood, Howard also takes a keen interest in what's going on inside the bodies of coral reef fish. For decades, biologists have believed that whole families of coral reef fishes were herbivores. After all, divers had observed these fish ingesting algae, and it seemed logical that this is what the fish were after. By studying the guts of fish and the food inside them, however, Howard has totally changed the way scientists think about coral reef fish feeding. He and his colleague Kendall Clements discovered that many different fishes considered to be herbivores actually get their nutrition from *microbes*, detritus, sea jellies, *crustaceans*, *crinoids*, *plankton*, other fish, and even fish waste materials!

"The interesting thing," Howard explains, "is that they all have an herbivore-based gut. They probably all started out as herbivores and used their herbivore gut to evolve all sorts of new, amazing feeding strategies."

Howard's discoveries have important implications for fisheries and reef management. Many of the long-lived fishes he has studied are prized by commercial fishers. Howard's data shows that if fishers target these species, it may be many years before those fish are replaced. His studies on so-called herbivores, on the other hand, show that their links to other reef animals are much more complex than people previously thought. If the animals that provide food for these fish are destroyed, damaging chain reactions could be set off in many parts of the reef ecosystem.

Howard has made many important contributions to science, but he still has many more questions he'd like to answer. "I'm driven by fundamental interest and curiosity," he explains. "I'm 62 now, and I intend to keep diving as long as I can because I'm committed to field-work. So every year, I go and make sure I pass my dive medical, and then I put on my gear and get back on the reef."

FOUR

Swim, Baby, Swim

Sixteen feet (5 m) below the ocean surface, Jeff Leis and Brooke Carson-Ewart float suspended in blue, open water. They couldn't be more vulnerable. Lizard Island sits more than half a mile (1 km) away, and the seafloor lies out of sight far beneath them. This is shark territory, not a place for two helpless humans, but this is exactly where the two scientists want to be.

After Brooke gives him the OK sign to confirm that she is ready, Jeff carefully removes the lid from a jar full of seawater. Inside swims the pushpin-sized larva of a butterflyfish. As soon as the lid is removed, the tiny fish darts out into the open ocean and starts swimming. With a kick of their fins, Jeff and Brooke begin their pursuit with nothing but blue water and light to protect them.

Jeff Leis is one of a handful of pioneers investigating the mysterious world of coral reef fish larvae. Like corals, most coral reef fish reproduce by spawning. They shed eggs and sperm into the water, and after the eggs are fertilized, they hatch into tiny "fishlets" known as larvae. As soon as they begin developing, however, most coral reef fish larvae are swept out to the open sea by ocean currents. This requires a larva to have very different equipment and adaptations than its parents.

Out in the open ocean, larvae eat different foods from adult reef fish. An adult butterflyfish, for example, feeds on live coral polyps and other reef invertebrates. Its young, on the other hand, hunt tiny planktonic animals such as copepods. Many larvae have unusually big eyes and heads that allow them to spot and swallow their prey.

Larvae also have to avoid being eaten by predators. In the open ocean, they have nothing to hide behind. Some larvae congregate under drifting logs or seaweed, but most depend on transparent or silvery bodies to camouflage them against the blue open water or the sky above. For added protection, many larvae come armed with exceptionally long, needlelike spines that make them difficult for a predator to swallow.

Even though the appearance and lives of larvae differ dramatically from their parents, it is the survival of the larvae that ultimately determines how many adult fish end up on a reef and where those fish live. Until recently, however, scientists knew almost nothing about fish larvae. They didn't know where the larvae went, what they did, or for many species, even what they looked like. Jeff Leis is one of several scientists who has dedicated his life to filling in the missing blanks about this crucial period in the lives of coral reef fishes.

A Biologist's Larval Phase

Jeff Leis first became interested in larval fishes while doing his Ph.D. at the University of Hawaii. "I'd been offered a research assistantship

At Lizard Island, Jeff Leis usually dives in the morning to run experiments. In the evening, he analyzes his data in one of the LIRS offices.

in the marine lab at the Hawaiian Institute of Marine Biology on Kaneohe Bay," Jeff recalls. "They told me to look at the projects they had underway and choose an assistantship with anyone I wanted. Well, the thing that sounded most interesting to me was a larval fish project that was connected to an *aquaculture* program. They were doing a survey of the bay to try to get an idea of when different larval fish could be found there. They thought they could collect fish eggs that were being spawned naturally and use them in aquaculture."

"That sounded very interesting to me," Jeff continues. "So while I was doing my first couple of years of coursework for my Ph.D., I worked on this project, and the more I got into it, the more interesting it seemed. Eventually, I decided to do research on fish larvae for my thesis."

For his Ph.D. thesis, Jeff chose to investigate a very practical problem—how the seawater cooling system of a power plant might harm fish larvae. As he worked, however, bigger questions about larvae cropped up in his mind. Jeff incorporated some of these into his thesis. After he graduated, Jeff was awarded a 2-year postdoctoral fellowship at the Australian Museum in Sydney. He's been conducting research on fish larvae at the museum ever since.

Fish Questions

Jeff's research has led him to tackle a wide variety of mysteries about larvae. In his earlier work, he focused on learning where fish larvae go from the time they hatch until the time they settle on the reef. To find out, he used nets and traps to capture larvae almost everywhere he could think of, from coral lagoons to the open ocean far offshore. What he discovered was that different larvae end up in different places at different times. Some cardinalfish larvae spend their entire lives in sheltered lagoons. Other larvae gather on the windward or leeward sides of reefs while still others—including many surgeonfishes, wrasses, and butterflyfishes—end up scattered throughout the Coral Sea and even hundreds of miles out into the Pacific.

It was the larvae he found far from the reef that intrigued Jeff the most. He wondered, "What are they doing out there?"

Jeff's studies and the studies of other researchers have shown that living far from the reef may offer several advantages to fish larvae, including safety. Coral reefs are full of predators. Dozens of kinds of adult reef fish feed on larvae; so do sea anemones, corals, and other sedentary hunters. Heading out to sea may give larvae a better chance to avoid being eaten than staying on the reef.

Sending larvae out to sea may also allow coral reef fishes to hedge their bets. If larvae always stay close to the home reef and a cyclone or other disaster destroys that reef, a fish population could be wiped out for good. However, if the larvae are scattered out at sea, some will probably end up settling and surviving on other reefs. Some might even colonize new habitats—such as new volcanic islands—and allow that species to extend its range.

For Jeff, however, an even bigger mystery remained. "Once these larvae go out to sea," he asked himself, "how do they make it *back?*"

Superfish

For many years, scientists assumed that fish larvae drift passively, going wherever ocean currents carry them. Many oceanographers and biologists spent years trying to explain how a fish larva could be born near a reef, get carried hundreds of miles away, and still make it back to the same or a different coral reef. The scientists came up with complex mathematical models and charted endless ocean currents, but none of their arguments convinced Jeff.

In the 1980s, Jeff and a number of other researchers observed that larvae seem to swim quite well, at least near the end of the their larval phase. Jeff thought that the larvae could probably swim to different depths in the ocean to catch currents going in different directions. Perhaps, he surmised, this is how they made it back to a reef.

Then, in 1997, one of David Bellwood's graduate students, Ilona Stobutzki, published an astonishing finding: not only can larval fish swim, as Jeff and others suspected, they can swim a lot! Ilona figured this out at Lizard Island by placing larval fish in little raceways with artificial water currents running through them. She made the fish swim until they gave up and then multiplied the time they had swum by the speed of the current in the raceway. Ilona found that far from being passive drifters, the fish often swam for days at a time—sometimes more than 60 miles (100 km) without a break! This startling discovery totally changed the way biologists view fish larvae and has helped spark new directions for larval fish research.

Coming Home

In recent years, Jeff has been building upon his previous studies and Ilona's findings. He wants to answer two questions: Do larval fish actually swim as much in the ocean as they do in an artificial raceway? and If so, how fast do they travel?

To find out, Jeff, Brooke, and their assistants took their boat just offshore of Lizard Island in the evening and placed special *light traps* in different places. These traps used a fluorescent lightbulb to lure larvae into a box they couldn't get out of. The next morning, the scientists pulled up the traps, sorted through the larvae, separated out the ones they wanted, and placed them in a plastic aquarium. Then, they loaded up their scuba gear and headed out to sea.

In 1995 and 1996, Jeff and Brooke made three trips to Lizard Island. They caught larvae from more than thirty-nine species of coral reef fishes and measured how fast they swam in open water. To do this, they got in the water carrying a jar that contained a larval fish. When both divers were ready, one person removed the top of the jar and released the fish.

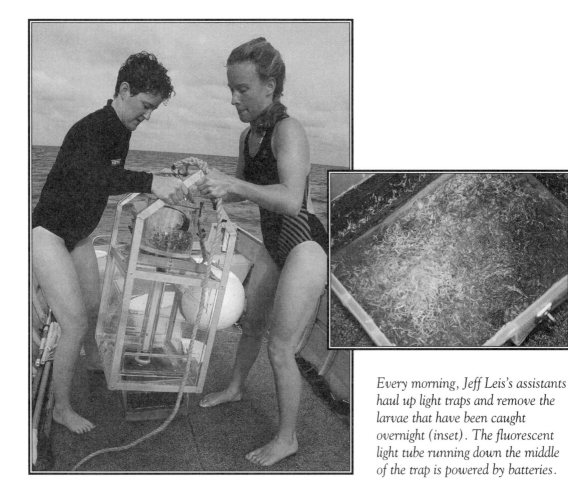

Every morning, Jeff Leis's assistants haul up light traps and remove the larvae that have been caught overnight (inset). The fluorescent light tube running down the middle of the trap is powered by batteries.

While one person kept his or her eye on the larva and followed it, the other person used a current meter to measure how fast the fish was swimming and also kept track of the diver'stime, depth, and direction. If the fish dove below 65 feet (20 m) deep, they halted the run because it would have endangered the divers. If the fish behaved "properly," however, they followed it for 10 minutes. Then they repeated the experiment with another fish.

Jeff and Brooke found enormous variations in the speeds of different larval fish. Some swam quite "pokily," traveling less than 1 inch

(2.5 cm) per second. Others turned out to be speed demons, swimming more than 24 inches (60 cm) per second. This was much faster than the ocean currents around them and, in terms of body-lengths, was the equivalent of a person swimming 54 miles (90 km) per hour! This was an important discovery because it proved not only that larval fish can swim, but that they *do*.

Have Compass, Will Travel

Jeff's next question was: Do the larvae actually know where the reef is? To find out, Jeff caught some more larval fish with light traps and took them to three different sites around Lizard Island. All of the sites were at least half a mile away from the nearest reef. He released the larvae and followed them, recording their swimming directions every 30 seconds. Of the sixty-six larvae he released, fifty-nine swam in definite directions and fifty-two spent more than half of their time swimming away from Lizard Island.

These observations told Jeff that the larval fish definitely seem to know where the reef is located. But why did they swim *away* from it? In later experiments, Jeff found that the larvae seemed to prefer swimming *toward* the reef. Jeff thinks this could have something to do with the time of day he ran the experiments.

In the daytime, larvae may want to stay away from the reef to avoid predators that could see them. At night, most larvae return to the reef to "settle." This could explain why the larvae in the second experiment were swimming toward the reef. Jeff hopes to learn more about larval swimming behavior as he conducts additional studies. He also hopes to answer an even bigger question: How do the larvae know where the reef is?

Lizard Island's Blue Lagoon offers scientists a calm place to work during storms and other inclement weather.

The tentacles of many corals only
come out to feed at night.

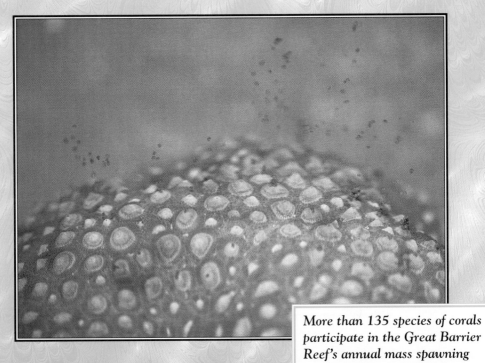

More than 135 species of corals participate in the Great Barrier Reef's annual mass spawning event. Two of those species are shown here.

Andrew Heyward's colleague Max Rees separates eggs (top layer) and sperm (bottom layer) in a beaker so that other scientists can conduct experiments on coral reproduction.

Anne Hoggett and Andrew Heyward celebrate the beginning of the annual mass spawning event.

For their studies, Andrew and his team keep coral larvae in these floating holding pens until they are ready to settle onto the reef.

LIRS's dive facilities make it easy for scientists to conduct underwater research.

Anne Hoggett hunts crown-of-thorns sea stars during a study of how best to control the thorny predator.

David Bellwood and his graduate student David Marne discuss strategies for another fish-filled dive.

David Bellwood removes a parrotfish from a handheld net.

Jeff Leis and Brooke Carson-Ewart select the fish larvae they want to "swim with" during an upcoming dive.

"The larvae tend to swim toward or away from the reef no matter what side of Lizard Island they're on," Jeff explains, "so we've eliminated the possibility that larvae use magnetism or the sun to find their way to the reef. That means we need to look at things like current, smell, and sound. First, we're going to look at sound. That seems to be the best possibility." To test his theory, Jeff plans to take larvae out into the open ocean and lower special speakers into the water. He will start playing "reef noises" that he has

Jeff Leis plans to hang speakers over the side of this inflatable boat to learn whether fish larvae are attracted to reef noises.

recorded and then release the larvae to see whether they head toward or away from the sounds. If the larvae swim toward or away from the speakers, it will be a good indication that larval fish can hear and that they respond to noises made by the reef.

Blue-Water Encounters

A special thrill of Jeff's research comes from the environment he and his colleagues work in. While most marine scientists work close to shore or in shallow water, Jeff and his team conduct their studies in open "blue" water with nothing to protect them. Over the years, Jeff and his colleague Brooke have had a number of encounters that let them know firsthand what a tiny fish larva must feel like.

"On our last trip to Lizard Island," Brooke recounts, "one of our assistants, Amanda Hay, and I were swimming in relatively murky water that was about 60 feet [18 m] deep. We were about 1 mile [1.5 km] from the beach. Amanda, who was following a larval fish, suddenly turned and faced me with very big eyes. I stopped and looked down just in time to see a large shark—6 to 10 feet [2 to 3 m] long—swimming about 15 feet [5 m] below us, following a large school of fish. It must have come up from behind us. Needless to say, we decided to call it a day and started slowly ascending. Once we realized that the shark wasn't interested in us, though, we dissolved into laughter and could barely speak by the time we got to the surface.

"The most exciting thing I have seen while doing this stuff—well the most exciting thing ever, I think—was while diving in blue water a couple of miles offshore of Rangiroa atoll in the South Pacific. Jeff and I had finished the last dive of the day and were very slowly ascending from about 65 feet [20 m] down. Jeff was madly writing notes on his slate and I was just looking around. The water was crystal clear, and I could see the boat from quite a distance away.

"Suddenly, I noticed a very large shape swim behind the boat and reappear on the other side. It was a blue marlin. As soon as it spotted us, it very slowly made its way over. It circled us, gave us a good looking over, and then slowly swam away. Distance is very hard to estimate in such clear water, but I'd guess it came within 30 feet [9 m] of us, and Jeff reckons it was bigger than I am—more than 6 feet [2 m] tall. Jeff told me later that marlins like to stab things—big things like logs and boats that they have no intention of eating. While I was watching the marlin, it never once occurred to me that it might be checking us out for a spot of sword fighting!"

Swimming Farther

The occasional shark or marlin encounter adds spice to Jeff and Brooke's work, but Jeff also enjoys the nuts and bolts of research. "I love the excitement of discovering new things and the fun of seeing how complex ecosystems work," he explains. I also love the variety and the challenge. Aside from this behavioral work, I've done a lot of taxonomy, trying to figure out what species the different larvae belong to. In many ways, it's like detective work matching up these different larvae to the adult fish. I also enjoy solving different problems that I encounter—little technical problems like how we're going to build a piece of equipment to answer a particular question or how we're going to fix a piece of gear that's broken."

Jeff and Brooke are not alone in their love of larval research. In the past few years, there has been a huge explosion of interest in reef larvae, what they do, and how they influence adult reef populations. "Some of the interest is because there was virtually nothing known before," Jeff explains. "People have gradually come to realize that the larval stage is a big part of the life cycles of these animals. If you just look at the adult fish and ignore their larval stages, your knowledge is incomplete and you'll never know what's really going on. In fact, some traditional approaches to studying fish populations and competition have come to a dead end. People are starting to believe that fish larvae could provide some of the answers they're looking for."

CORAL REEF BRIEF

Common Interests

Many researchers share Jeff Leis's interest in the early life stages of fishes. As more and more people recognize the importance of the early stages in fishes' lives, biologists have begun to look at all aspects of juvenile fish ecology and their effects on adult fish populations. Two of these researchers are Brigid Kerrigan and Mark McCormick.

Brigid and Mark work independently but share a common heritage. Both are "Kiwis"—they were born and raised in New Zealand. There, they began working on temperate, or cool-water, fishes. In the mid-1980s, both came to Australia as part of a "Kiwi invasion" led by New Zealander Howard Choat. Now, both conduct research at Lizard Island on the early life stages of damselfishes.

Bringing Up Baby

Brigid, who was raised on a New Zealand sheep ranch, focuses on how maternal influences might affect the survival of damselfish larvae. For these studies, she works on a damselfish called the spiny chromis, *Acanthochromis polyacanthus*. Most damselfishes are *benthic spawners*. The females lay their eggs in nests. When a male arrives, he fertilizes the eggs and then guards them until they hatch. Afterward, the larvae disperse away from the reef for several weeks before returning to settle down.

Originally from New Zealand, Brigid Kerrigan studies how a mother fish's health affects the health and survival of her young.

The spiny chromis, however, has a different reproductive pattern. After the larvae hatch, they stay on the reef in tight little balls, or schools, and are guarded by both parents in a depression or shallow cave until they grow larger. Because the larvae do not disperse, Brigid can study the fish's entire reproductive process from start to finish.

In early experiments, Brigid set up artificial patch reefs—small chunks of coral—just offshore from Lizard Island. She placed a breeding female damselfish on each patch reef. In her first experiment, Brigid fed half of the females extra food and let the other females find their own food. When the females laid their eggs and the larvae hatched, Brigid looked at them to see if she could find any differences between the two groups of young. She discovered that the "fed females"—the ones she gave extra food—produced larger eggs with more yolk and that their larvae were bigger and healthier, too. This told Brigid that the health of a mother fish may play a big role in the survival of her young.

Currently, Brigid is building on those results by feeding damselfish mothers and then watching to see if their young grow faster and survive better than if they'd had "unfed" mothers. When the young hatch, Brigid tags them by injecting a colorful substance called *elastomer* under their scales. These bright tags allow Brigid to identify individual fish when she returns to Lizard Island to check on their progress.

Fish Food

Mark McCormick also uses elastomer to tag damselfish, but he is trying to answer different questions than Brigid. Mark wants to get a handle on *post-settlement mortality*—the rate at which young fish die after they settle on the reef. "People think that larval mortality is pretty high, but few people have documented it," Mark explains. "We're trying to get really good data on how high mortality is and what determines it. Is it related to the quality of the environment, the number of shelter sites, or how much coral grows at a particular place?"

In his experiments, Mark uses light traps to collect damselfish larvae and then divides the larvae into groups of twenty fish each. He places or "settles" these groups onto different patch reefs. He leaves some of the reefs open and exposed to predators and encloses others with cages that have different sized mesh openings in them. The cages let different sizes and kinds of predators reach the larvae. This setup allows Mark to keep track of how many larvae get eaten and which ones get eaten first.

Mark McCormick was one of the first biologists to measure survival rates of young fish after they return to settle on the reef.

Mark focuses his studies on the Ambon damselfish, *Pomacentrus amboinensis*. "Pom amboinensis has a very typical life cycle for a reef fish, and that's why we're studying it," Mark explains. "After hatching, the larvae disperse off the reef for 16 to 21 days and then return to the reef as bright yellow juveniles." Unlike many other species, however, the Ambon damselfish settles in very high numbers most years, making it easier to study than more "unreliable" species.

Larvae Lessons

Both Brigid and Mark have made some surprising discoveries. Brigid's studies are still underway, but she says,

"Fish from well-fed parents appear to have a higher growth rate and, initially, their broods are larger. But these juveniles stay in a tight ball, and I have the feeling that the larger groups of young attract more predators, so I'm not sure that larger brood sizes necessarily provide a survival advantage."

As Mark expected, his research shows that fatter, better-nourished young survive better than smaller young on his patch reefs. What he didn't expect was the intensity of predation throughout his study area. "Mortality is very high," Mark explains. "In 2 days, we lost 50 percent of our fish on many of the patch reefs." What was most startling, however, was that mortality in the fine-mesh cages—the ones Mark thought would offer the most protection—was often as high as or higher than predation in the big-mesh or open cages.

"Some of the small predators that got into the fine-mesh cages just hammered the young fish," Mark says. "But interestingly enough, in some of the open cages, large adult male damselfish moved in. They are very territorial. They built nests and beat the crap out of wrasses and other predators. In one of the open cages, 90 percent of the young survived, while in some of the fine-meshed cages, only 2 percent survived. Apparently, in addition to size and health, survival also depends on where young fish take up residence."

FIVE

Reef Relationships

THOUSANDS OF KINDS OF ORGANISMS LIVE ON THE GREAT BARRIER Reef, but it is not just their individual stories that make the reef so interesting. Scientists are also fascinated by the relationships *between* species. The Great Barrier Reef is a highly interdependent world, where species interact and rely on each other in ways that we are barely beginning to understand.

Some of these interactions are truly startling, such as the relationship between corals and their zooxanthellae. Equally intriguing is the link between algae and the reef as a whole. Although corals provide the raw material for reef construction, algae fuse dead corals, sand, and rubble to form a solid structure. Without these algae, the reef would never form. Other interesting reef relationships involve fish. Clownfishes and sea anemones live peacefully together, while cleaner wrasses provide an important service for a variety of other fishes.

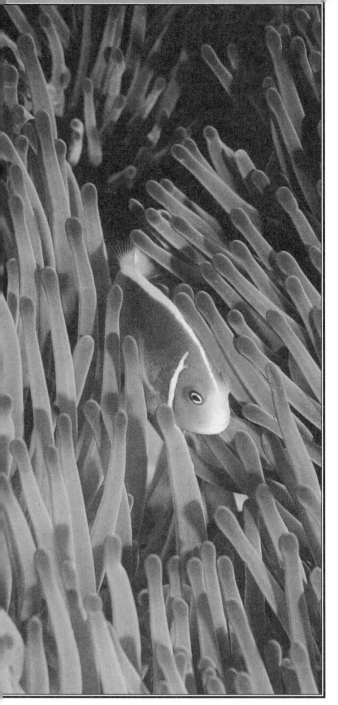

The mutualistic relationship between the clownfish and its poisonous anemone host has fascinated biologists and divers for years.

Clownin' Around

Twenty-seven species of clownfishes, or anemonefishes, live on the world's reefs, from the Caribbean and Red Seas to the eastern South Pacific. Few divers see a clownfish without being charmed by its bright colors and curious, bold behavior. What's most amazing about these fishes, however, are their relationships with their sea anemone hosts.

Clownfish make their homes among the deadly tentacles of sea anemones. Although most kinds of fish are quickly stung to death by these tentacles, a clownfish moves freely in and out of the waving, spaghetti-like stingers. Scientists believe that this arrangement is an example of *mutualism*—a relationship between two species that benefits both of them. For the clownfish, the benefits are obvious. The poisonous sea anemone protects the clownfish from bigger fish and other predators. The benefit to the sea anemone is less clear, but scientists speculate that the clownfish chases away butterflyfishes and other animals that nip bites out of the anemone's tentacles.

One question crops up again and again: Why doesn't the sea anemone sting the clownfish to death? Scientists still aren't sure of the answer. Some believe that the mucus on a clownfish's skin doesn't contain the chemicals that trigger a sea anemone's stingers. Others believe that the clownfish chemically disguises itself by carefully rubbing against the mucus of the sea anemone. Whichever explanation is correct, one thing is certain: without sea anemones, clownfish would never survive.

Like most other coral reef fishes, clownfish spend the first weeks of their lives as tiny larvae out in the open sea. When they return to the reef to settle down, how do they know which kinds of anemones to settle down with—or even that they should seek out an anemone at all? These are two questions biologist Michael Arvedlund has been attempting to answer.

Are You My Mother?

Michael Arvedlund was born in Denmark, only a few miles from the North Sea. Like David Bellwood, he took an avid interest in aquariums as a child. "When I was 8 years old," he recounts, "my father died in an accident working for a cement company, and my mother's uncle began spending time with me, introducing me to various hobbies. He had a lot of fish tanks and took me down to one of the aquarium shops in Copenhagen. We walked in and suddenly, thirty big tanks full of corals and coral reef fish confronted me and it was like, 'Wow!'"

When Michael turned 12, his mother gave him a coral reef tank, and he began keeping live corals and various coral reef fish. "I was really in love with them," he remembers. "I ended up doing some damselfish breeding [clownfishes are types of damselfishes] and even managed to get some young, but I didn't know how to care for them, and they didn't survive."

When he graduated from high school, Michael was accepted into Copenhagen University, but another interest took his life on a sharp detour—ballroom dancing. A dancer from the age of 10, Michael joined the Danish national team and decided to postpone college, at least for the time being. "I sold everything," he explains, "and left school for 3 or 4 years. I performed in Denmark and then moved to London, where I tried to establish myself as a ballroom dancer. I ended up reaching number 48 or something on the world rank list, but I was very immature and young. I was always fighting with other people, including my girlfriend and dance partner. After 2 years, I gave it up and went back to Denmark to take classes at the university.

"At first," he recalls, "I just took the required courses and didn't really know what interested me. Then one day, I walked by an aquarium shop and said to myself, 'Ah! I remember that! I was keen on that!' And I took it up again."

After completing his undergraduate degree in zoology, Michael earned a master's degree and began working on one of the animals he had raised as a boy—the clownfish. Afterward, the Danish government awarded him a scholarship to complete a Ph.D. at James Cook University in Townsville, Australia.

A Nose for Survival

One of the early questions Michael asked about clownfish was whether they detected sea anemones by sight or by smell. Scientists had already determined that sea anemones release a strong chemical "perfume" that a clownfish can detect. However, no one had ever proved that clownfish use this perfume to locate their anemone hosts.

To answer this question, Michael set up a series of experiments in aquariums. He raised clownfish eggs with and without their sea anemone hosts. When the clownfish larvae hatched, Michael separated them and kept the larvae and the anemones in different aquariums. After the fish matured, he began reintroducing them to the anemones to see what would happen.

The first thing Michael learned was that clownfish definitely find sea anemones by smell. When Michael allowed clownfish to see an anemone through glass—but not smell any of the water the anemone was in—the clownfish didn't recognize the anemone. If Michael added even a tiny bit of water from the anemone's aquarium, however, the clownfish immediately swam to the source of that water.

In this study, however, Michael was also trying to answer a second question: Do young clownfish *imprint* on their hosts?

For his Ph.D. research, Michael Arvedlund has tried to unravel the mysteries of the clownfish-anemone relationship.

Imprinting is well-known in birds and other animals. Baby geese that are raised by a person, for instance, will consider that person to be their parent for the rest of their lives. Michael wondered whether clownfish might do the same thing.

To find out, he took the clownfish he'd raised in isolation and placed them in aquariums with sea anemones. When he did this, the clownfish initially ignored the anemones. They did eventually acclimate to their sea anemone hosts, but it took them about 2 days. However, clownfish that hatched from eggs raised in the presence of sea anemones immediately swam over to the anemones and "settled in" to their mutualistic relationship. These findings indicate that clownfish can chemically imprint on anemones even before they hatch.

Clowns Continued

After his early experiments, Michael conducted many other studies to learn more about clownfish-anemone relationships. One thin he tried was to get clownfishes to imprint on sea anemones that were not their usual hosts. Most clownfishes live with only one or two species of sea anemones. Michael wondered, Could he get clownfishes to live in a mutualistic relationship with different anemone species?

He discovered that the answer was "No." Clownfishes are reluctant to get involved with new species of sea anemones. This showed Michael that a clownfish's relationship with its sea anemone host is at least partly "hardwired" into its genetic code. From his lab experiments, however, Michael also knew that the relationship could be reinforced by imprinting. Next, he asked himself, Does this imprinting actually take place out on the reef?

To find out, he conducted two field surveys, one in the Red Sea and the other around Lizard Island. During nesting seasons, Michael swam around the reefs and looked for clownfish to see where they were laying their eggs. What he found helped confirm what he had learned in the lab.

In both the Red Sea and the Great Barrier Reef, the vast majority of clownfish lay their eggs directly above their sea anemone hosts. This allows ocean currents to carry a sea anemone's chemicals over the eggs and even allows the sea anemone tentacles to rub against the eggs. Michael concluded that the most likely explanation for this is that it helps reinforce imprinting on the developing clownfish. This stronger imprinting, in turn, increases the survival rate of young clownfish when they return to the reef and look for an anemone to settle down with.

One more piece of the puzzle was still missing, however. No one had ever proved that young clownfish can smell! And if they can't smell, then Michael would have to throw all his theories out the window. As one last project for his Ph.D., Michael used high-powered electron microscopes to look at the *olfactory*, or smelling, organs of young clownfish. He discovered that even as larvae, clownfish have well-developed olfactory organs. Michael cautions that this doesn't mean that larvae definitely can smell, but it provides strong evidence that young clownfish are able to sniff out anemone hosts.

May I Check Your Gills?

The clownfish-anemone relationship is far from the only example of mutualism on the coral reef. When Alexandra Grutter worked as a diving guide in Hawaii in the mid-1980s, she loved showing other divers the underwater cleaning stations. The stations were run by tiny, striped fish called cleaner wrasses. The wrasses would set up shop by a rock or large piece of coral and bigger fish—the customers—would line up to get cleaned one at a time.

To get cleaned, the customer would strike a pose and then one or two cleaner fish would swarm all over it, picking *parasites* off the customer's skin. The cleaner fish went up and down the customer's body and even swam inside its gills and mouth. Each time Alexandra, or "Lexa," watched these hardworking fish, she asked herself all kinds of questions: Why did the customer fish want to be cleaned so much? Did cleaning actually help the customer fish? What benefits, if any, did the cleaner wrasses get out of the deal? It would be several years before Lexa could begin to find the answers.

After working as a diving guide, Lexa decided to study marine biology at the University of Hawaii and, later, at the University of California at Santa Barbara. Afterward, she won a full scholarship to do her Ph.D. at James Cook University. Meanwhile, she kind of forgot about cleaner fish. One day, though, she mentioned to Howard Choat and David Bellwood that she had worked in Hawaii, where a lot of cleaner fish studies had been done. David Bellwood told Lexa that, by coincidence, he had taken an interest in the mouth structures of cleaner fish. As they talked, Lexa suddenly found her "cleaner fish curiosity" growing all over again.

I'll Clean Your Back If . . .

When Lexa started studying cleaner fish, scientists had many conflicting opinions about the cleaners' importance to other coral reef fish. One early study indicated that without cleaner fish, other fish suffer

Until Alexandra Grutter began working on cleaner fish (far right), no one knew for sure how important the cleaners are in keeping other fish parasite-free.

from excessive numbers of parasites. Other research suggested that cleaner fish don't affect parasite numbers one way or the other. Still other studies showed that cleaner fish really don't eat many parasites at all, but feed mainly on mucus. Lexa decided to begin sorting out this complicated, conflicting story.

"The main objective of my work is to figure out why fish get cleaned," she says. "What is the purpose of cleaning? Is it mutualistic? Do both parties benefit?"

Earlier studies had shown that cleaner fish in Hawaii feed mostly on mucus, so this seemed a good place for Lexa to start her research. When she studied cleaner fish on the Great Barrier Reef, however, she discovered that they behave differently from their Hawaiian counterparts. "I spent my first year looking at mucus-feeding," Lexa explains. "But when I started looking at the guts of cleaner fish on the Great Barrier Reef, they were so full of parasites, it made no sense to look at the mucus."

With this realization, Lexa shifted her focus to parasites, especially a kind of *gnathiid isopod* that feeds on a wide variety of coral reef fish and seems to be a favorite target of cleaner fish. With help from her husband and dive buddy Mark, Lexa began trying to get a handle on how many gnathiid isopods, or gnathiids, one cleaner fish eats in a day. She spent hundreds of hours underwater, observing cleaner fish feed and catching them to see what was in their stomachs. From this work, Lexa came up with an astonishing conclusion: in 1 day, a single cleaner fish eats up to 1,200 gnathiids! Not only that, but gnathiids seem to be the fishes' main source of food. These discoveries set the groundwork for her next investigations.

All Aboard the Parasite Train!

Lexa wondered whether the actions of the cleaner fish affect the numbers of parasites on other reef fish. Earlier studies had looked at this problem by removing cleaner fish from one set of reefs and leaving them on another set. Scientists monitored the numbers of parasites feeding on various species of reef fishes, but after 2 years, they found no differences between the two reefs. Lexa, however, suspected that the cleaner fish *do* affect parasite numbers. She thought she might have to carry out studies for an even longer period of time before she'd see those effects. This was not something she looked forward to! But then, she made a fortunate observation.

"To make sure I wouldn't lose anything, I started collecting fish in zip-lock plastic bags," she recalls. "As soon as I caught a fish, I'd pop it in a bag and seal it up. One day I was looking in the bag at a fish I'd just caught, and I saw a little black thing swimming around. It was a gnathiid isopod. I'd just taken the fish out of the water and already this parasite had jumped off the fish. That's when I realized that these parasites are really mobile."

This observation transformed how Lexa thought about the parasite-cleaner relationship. Previously, scientists had assumed that the benefits of cleaner fish occurred gradually over long periods of time. Now, Lexa began thinking they might happen very quickly. To find out, she collected various reef fishes from dawn to sunset. She found that the fishes had twice as many gnathiids at dawn as at dusk. Was this a result of the way the parasites behaved—or was it because the cleaner fish were removing parasites during the day?

To find out, Lexa began conducting a variety of experiments on the reefs around Lizard Island. In one experiment, she placed parasite-free fish in cages underwater and looked at how quickly and when parasites jumped onto them during the next 24 hours. In a similar experiment, she put fish in underwater cages with and without cleaner fish and

At Lizard Island, Lexa has been conducting long-term studies on parasites and the fish they attack.

monitored parasite numbers for a 24-hour period. Her results revolutionized the way scientists view cleaner fish.

Cleanin' Up

In her first caging experiment, Lexa found that within a few hours of placing her "clean fish" underwater, they became fully loaded with parasites. This startled her because no one had believed that the parasites could attack fish so quickly. She also found that gnathiids attack fish at all times of the day and night instead of only at night, as other scientists had suggested. This means that the behavior of the gnathiids does not explain why there are more parasites on fish at dawn than at dusk.

Lexa's most exciting discovery, however, came from her second experiment. In this experiment, she found that the fish in cages without cleaner fish had four-and-a-half times more parasites than the fish in cages with cleaner fish.

These results showed for the first time that cleaner fish have a real, significant impact on the parasite loads of other fish. The results also indicated that customer fish get real benefits from being cleaned—a conclusion supported by how often customers visit the cleaning stations. From her observations underwater, Lexa has calculated that an average coral reef fish gets cleaned about 50,000 times each year—strong evidence that "keeping clean" is a good thing.

A Cleaner Future

When she started her cleaner fish work, Lexa thought she'd just find out a few things about cleaners and then move on to something else. Now, as a full-time researcher at the University of Queensland, she has so many questions about cleaner fish that she may just stick with them to learn more. "When I finished my Ph.D.," she explains, "I was pretty sick of cleaner fish, but after a vacation I went back to them and now I just think, 'Oh, there's so many more things to do. I'll just keep doing it.'"

For example, she'd like to investigate the behavior between cleaner fish and their customers. Often, cleaner fish clean big potato cod and other fishes that are thousands of times bigger than they are. Lexa wonders why the bigger fish don't eat the cleaner fish.

She'd also like to study cleaner fish that "cheat." Even though most cleaner fish eat parasites, Lexa has observed many that nip off bits of skin, mucus, scales, and fins from bigger fish. How do the cleaner fish know how much they can get away with before the bigger fish will make a meal of them?

As Lexa continues her work, she helps us understand more about some of the reef's most beloved characters. Her studies, though, also make us aware of the complexity of the reef and, in doing so, give us a greater respect for the delicate balance nature and evolution have achieved.

CORAL REEF BRIEF

Condos and Copycats

As remarkable as clownfish and cleaner wrasses are, they are only two of many creatures that have evolved close relationships with other reef animals. In his research, biologist Philip Munday has focused on another special reef relationship, the one between coral reef gobies and their living homes.

Goby Central

Approximately thirteen species of coral-dwelling gobies live on the Great Barrier Reef. Small, colorful fish, they are often overlooked by divers because they live among the protective treelike branches of certain kinds of corals. What fascinates Phil about these fish is that they are habitat-specialized. Each kind of goby lives almost exclusively in only one or two species of corals.

"They're quite similar to anemonefish [clownfish] that only live in one or two kinds of sea anemones," Phil explains. "Anemonefish are much more widely known, but gobies are actually much more abundant and diverse on coral reefs. I'm looking at them because I'm interested in whether habitat availability—in this case corals—helps determine the populations and distribution of coral gobies and other habitat-specialized fishes."

Through his research at Lizard Island and in Papua New Guinea, Phil has definitely found a relationship. "On a local scale," he explains, "there's no doubt that habitat equals abundance. If you have a crown-of-thorns outbreak or other event that kills corals, you get a dramatic drop in the numbers of gobies. The gobies don't just go find another coral and live in

Phil Munday decided to become a biologist while managing recreational dive centers in Papua New Guinea and the Maldive Islands.

big social groups. They disappear. We don't really know why they won't form larger social groups, but we're starting to investigate those things."

Phil's work is important because until recently, many scientists assumed that populations of reef fish were mostly determined by single, dominant factors. These included competition, predation, and recruitment—the numbers of young animals settling onto the reef each year. "Now," Phil says. "I think it's becoming obvious that many processes influence fish populations. What we need to learn is which fishes are influenced by which processes—and which processes operate at which scales."

Julian Caley's work with puffers and leather-jackets has shown that mimicry can increase a fish's protection from predators.

Fish Fakes

Phil works closely with Julian Caley, another biologist from James Cook University. Like Phil, Julian is interested in determining what influences populations, but over much wider areas. Again, relationships between species seem to be an important factor. Some of Julian's most intriguing work, however, concerns a different kind of relationship: *mimicry*.

Mimicry happens when one species, known as a mimic, evolves to look or behave like another species, known as a model. Usually, mimicry offers some protection for the mimic. A number of caterpillars, for instance, can make their hind ends look like the heads of venomous snakes. When a hungry bird approaches, these caterpillars raise up their "snake heads" and frighten the birds away.

The Great Barrier Reef contains many examples of mimicry, including the sharpnosed puffer and its mimic, the leatherjacket. "Sharpnosed puffers are very toxic. Predators such as big cods and wrasses leave them alone," Julian explains. "Fish called leatherjackets mimic the puffers, and what we wanted to do is look closely at the advantages for these mimics."

Julian wanted to know how good a mimic has to be to gain some protection. In other words, if a fish looks only a little bit like its poisonous model, will it get a little bit of protection, a lot of protection, or none at all?

Working with his Canadian colleague Dolph Schluter, Julian made plastic fishing lures that had the same body forms as sharpnosed puffers and leatherjackets. He then painted the lures. He painted some to look a lot like sharpnosed puffers, and others to look only a little like them.

"Then," says Julian, "Dolph and I went out onto the reef and fished. We looked at how many times the predators attacked the different lures, and we found that predators tended to avoid lures that looked even a little bit like the model. In other words, an animal doesn't have to be a perfect mimic to gain protection. The protection begins even when a mimic is physically quite different from the model."

Julian's "fishing trip" provides an interesting look into the relationships between predators and prey on the Great Barrier Reef. Even more interesting, it gives us insights into the processes that have led to coral reef evolution and diversity—processes that continue to this day.

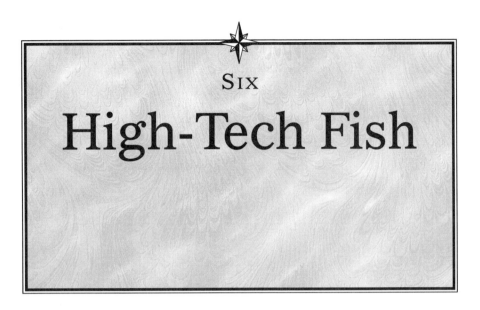

SIX

High-Tech Fish

Dirk Zeller felt perplexed. Using an underwater receiver hung over the side of his boat, he'd been tracking two coral trout he'd implanted with small ultrasonic transmitters. The signals from the fish were coming in loud and clear, but the trout were behaving strangely. Instead of moving around a small home range and then "bedding down" for the night, they'd been continuously roaming over a large area 24 hours a day. Not only that, the signals from both fish seemed to be coming from exactly the same places. From what Dirk knew about coral trout, this was highly unusual. Unless they were spawning, coral trout led solitary lives and were rarely found together. "What's going on?" he asked himself.

To find out, he followed the signals until he was right on top of them. Then, he asked his assistant to put on his mask and snorkel and leap over the side. Dirk expected his assistant to find the two coral trout, but instead, he landed directly over a 6-foot- (2-m) long white-tipped reef shark. Startled, the shark darted away, but in its belly it carried both of Dirk's fish and his $800 transmitters. Over the next few days, Dirk tried everything he could think of to catch the shark and retrieve his transmitters, but the shark outsmarted him. In the end, Dirk had to chalk up the loss to the learning process and the cost of investigating one of the Great Barrier Reef's most important resources.

From Cousteau to the Coral Sea

Part of what makes marine science so fascinating is that it often involves more than answering biological questions. Because marine science requires working in an unfamiliar, often hostile environment, it frequently demands thinking up new ways of answering questions and solving complex technical problems. For scientists such as Dirk Zeller, this technical side of marine research can be just as rewarding as the biology.

Dirk grew up in Germany's Black Forest, where he developed a passionate interest in animals. As a child, he rode horses and kept dogs, squirrels, and cats as pets. "But as a kid," he explains, "I always watched Jacques Cousteau on television, so scuba diving in the ocean became a big dream. When I was 18, I decided that I wanted to go on my own vacation, so I worked for a summer to earn money and then went to the Mediterranean, where I took a diving course. After that, I just wanted to know more about what was going on down there underwater."

Dirk finished high school in 1981 and spent the next 18 months as a paratrooper, fulfilling the national service required of all German citizens. Afterward, he traveled to Spain and Portugal to work as a scuba instructor, but his real passion remained biology. The problem was, he couldn't afford the college education required to pursue his passion. But then Dirk recalled a conversation he'd had several years earlier: "One day after I graduated from high school, I was driving home, and I picked up a hitchhiker who turned out to be from Sydney, Australia. I told him what I wanted to do and he said, 'Why don't you try Australia? Universities are free, and all these cities and universities are on the coastline. I'm sure someone does marine science.'"

Several years later, Dirk decided to take the hitchhiker's advice. He wrote to several Australian universities and expressed his desire to study marine science. They all wrote back and told him the same thing: go to James Cook University. So, in 1983, Dirk flew to Australia to start his undergraduate degree in zoology and marine biology. After graduating, he completed an honors thesis and then began his Ph.D. That's when he first became interested in coral trout and other fishes in the grouper family. It's also when he began working at Lizard Island.

Ecology and Technology

"I always had an interest in pure behavior of animals—what animals do and why," he explains. "So I wanted to do something that focused on that, but I also wanted to do something with a practical application because I'm interested in applied fisheries issues and environmental issues in relation to fisheries."

Dirk recognized that even though many larger Great Barrier Reef fishes are important economically, fisheries biologists knew almost nothing about how they behave or why they move from place to place. "The vast majority of research has been on tiny little fish," Dirk says.

"That's because you can catch little fish more easily, and they tend to stay in one place where you can easily observe them. But I wanted to look at bigger fish, especially commercial species."

Dirk decided to try his hand at tracking individual fish around Lizard Island by using a technique called *ultrasonic telemetry*. This involves attaching ultrasonic transmitters to animals and following their underwater movements with a special receiver mounted on a boat. People had used ultrasonic telemetry to track sharks, whales, and salmon, but no one had succeeded in using it on Australian coral reef fish. Still, Dirk figured that he could get the system up and running in a few months.

The task turned out to be more difficult than he had anticipated. One of his main obstacles was deciding where to put the transmitter. "There are three different methods for attaching a transmitter to a fish," Dirk explains. "You can attach it externally, force-feed it into the fish's stomach, or surgically sew it into the fish's body cavity. I tried force-feeding first, but the fish spit it out after a couple of hours or days. External attachments also didn't work. As the coral trout swam in and out of corals, they tried to rub the transmitters off. So my only option was surgical implants. I had to learn to be an animal surgeon very quickly."

Dirk began by catching a trout with a fishing pole, anesthetizing the fish, and then cutting open the fish's belly using surgical scissors. After he inserted the transmitter, he closed up the body cavity using surgical staples and then released the fish back onto the reef. The first three fish he operated on were all eaten by sharks. At first, Dirk didn't know why. He guessed, though, that he had not given the trout enough time to recover from surgery. When he released the trout, they probably

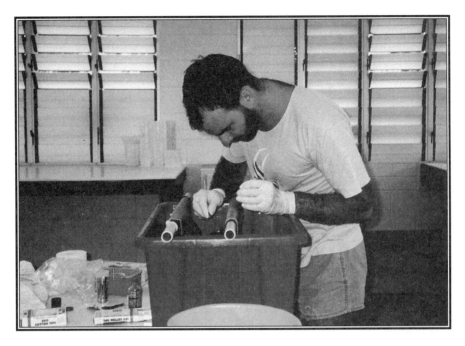

One of the keys to Dirk Zeller's research was learning how to safely implant his transmitters into coral trout.

sent out "injured" signals to sharks, which quickly located them and wolfed them down along with Dirk's costly transmitters.

After losing his first three fish, Dirk began giving the trout several days to recover from surgery. Then, one day when he was planning to insert some transmitters in fish, an Australian surgeon happened to be visiting Lizard Island. The surgeon asked if he could watch Dirk's technique, and Dirk said, "Sure." After watching Dirk, the surgeon suggested that instead of stapling the fish closed, he should try sewing them up with surgical thread. This would allow the fish to heal more rapidly. The surgeon even sent Dirk a whole box of operating supplies, including sutures. The technique worked flawlessly. Healing times dropped in half and after that, the vast majority of fish survived Dirk's operation and behaved normally on the reef.

Trout on the Move

Once he released the fish back onto the reef, Dirk was able to track their movements using a receiver attached to a microphone in the water. He was also ready to begin answering some questions about the secret lives of coral trout.

"There were quite a few questions related to movement of commercial reef fishes that needed addressing," Dirk explains, "particularly with large reef fishes. Are they active mostly in the daytime, at night, or both? How big is a trout's home range—the area where a fish spends most of its time? We also wanted to learn about movements related to the coral trout's *spawning aggregations*."

Dirk decided to begin by looking at the first two questions. He and an assistant released between five and fifteen trout onto the reef at a time and monitored them continuously. "On the first field trip, we monitored them for 3 weeks, 24 hours per day," Dirk recalls. "From that, I learned that the fish sleep at night, so thank goodness, I could begin sleeping again! Then we changed the whole project, and I concentrated on daytime tracking only."

Dirk spent 2 to 3 months at a time on Lizard Island, following his fish. The trout, he discovered, are generally homebodies. To survive, each trout stakes out a hunting ground, or home range, the size of a couple of football fields. Within that range, they slowly swim around looking for prey. When they spot a target, they stalk their prey like a lion, sneaking up close before a final, very fast rush. Dirk found, however, that the trout only travel about 650 feet (200 m) a day. At night,

Baby clownfish instinctively know to seek out an anemone when they settle on the coral reef.

Alexandra Grutter has spent hundreds of hours underwater observing cleaner wrasses and their relationships with the fish they clean.

Coral-dwelling gobies come in an astounding variety of colors, but they all need to live with particular kinds of corals to survive. Three species of gobies are shown here.

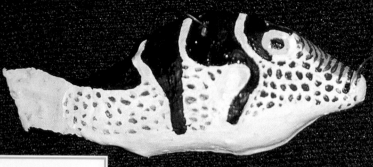

To study mimicry, Julian Caley and Dolph Schluter painted fishing lures to resemble sharpnosed puffers. Then, they went fishing.

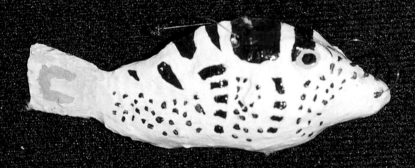

Dirk Zeller prepares LIRS's new automatic telemetry system for tracking fish in his "marine reserve" study.

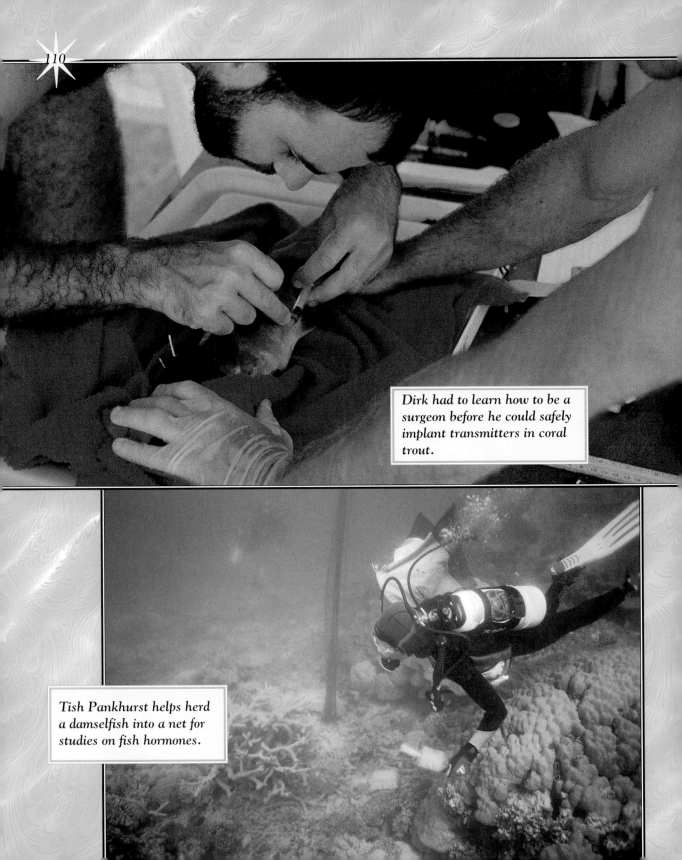

Dirk had to learn how to be a surgeon before he could safely implant transmitters in coral trout.

Tish Pankhurst helps herd a damselfish into a net for studies on fish hormones.

The author, Sneed B. Collard III, accompanied Lizard Island biologists on many dives. This helped him to better understand their research.

LIRS boats float peacefully
in the light of an Australian
sunset.

Dirk Zeller's tracking studies have shown that coral trout, such as this one, usually stick to a fairly small home range.

the fish return to the same spots on the reef, probably holes or overhangs that offer them protection from predators.

Breaking Away

Dirk discovered that coral trout break their homebody patterns when it comes to spawning. "A lot of coral reef fishes form spawning aggregations," Dirk explains. "Individual fish come together in the same place at the same time to release their eggs and sperm into the water, usually during a new or full moon. We know very little about these gatherings. We don't know where the fish come from, how long they stay there, or how far they disperse afterward."

By talking to other divers and following fish with transmitters, Dirk has been able to locate four coral trout spawning sites around Lizard

Island. By following fish to these sites, Dirk has learned that some coral trout travel long distances to spawn—often between 700 and 16,000 feet (220 and 4,900 m). Three of the fish Dirk monitored traveled 2, 5, and 7 miles (3, 8, and 11 km) respectively, indicating that coral trout can and do travel between reefs. Dirk counted up to sixty fish at a time at a spawning site and found that males stay at the sites about nine times longer than females. Many fish stay at the sites overnight, and most use the spawning sites closest to their home ranges time after time.

New Thinking

Using ultrasonic tracking, Dirk began filling in a huge area of knowledge about one of the Great Barrier Reef's most important game fish. His work also highlighted the dangers of fishing at spawning sites—a common practice on many coral reefs around the world. Commercial fishers can easily catch large quantities of fish at a spawning site, but this practice can quickly wipe out a fish population from a wide area. This is something reef managers need to consider when establishing fishing regulations.

Dirk's findings can be applied to other fish species as well. Now that he has worked out techniques for tracking coral trout, he and other biologists can use similar methods to track other important game fish such as snappers, emperors, and non-coral-trout grouper species.

Recently, Lizard Island acquired a stationary tracking system that can be set up on a coral reef and automatically record the positions of many tagged fish at one time. Dirk is especially excited about this new equipment because it will allow him to look at the finer points of how fish behave during spawning. Dirk wants to learn more about the different behaviors of males and females at a spawning site because he thinks that spawning may allow fish to evaluate numbers of males and females nearby. Coral trout, like many reef fish, are gender-changers. They are born females, but when they reach a certain size, they turn into males. Dirk thinks that when fish get together to spawn, females can somehow sense whether it is a good time to change into a male.

Dirk would also like to use the new tracking system to follow movements of many coral reef fish between areas. This has direct applications to coral reefs in the Philippines and other places that are heavily overfished. To help fish recover in these areas, reef managers are trying to set up protected *marine reserves*. The thinking is that if managers protect one part of the reef and allow fish to reproduce safely there, their young will spread to replenish other parts of the reef. The problem with this thinking is that no one has ever tested it. Because no one has ever actually counted how many fish move into and out of marine reserves, scientists don't know if the entire concept really works.

"To help answer this question," Dirk says, "we set up four areas at Lizard Island and have spent the last 2 years collecting information about the movements and distributions of a wide range of fish species. We haven't done any actual tracking yet, but the new equipment will allow us to release fish with transmitters and follow their smaller-scale movements."

Specifically, Dirk and his colleagues plan to remove some of the fish from two sites to simulate overfished areas. Then, they will follow the remaining fish to see where they go. They will also monitor the movements of fish in the sites designated as "protected reserves" to see where they go. The results will tell the scientists whether marine reserves sucessfully protect fish populations. They will also help reef managers develop more effective strategies for restoring coral reef fish populations.

CORAL REEF BRIEF

Hormones Down Under

Tish Pankhurst, Polly Hilder, and Mark Hilder swim above the reef waving big white bottle brushes below them. Ned Pankhurst, Tish's husband and research colleague, jokingly calls these giant brushes "coral probes." The scientists are using the probes to herd a damselfish into the 16-foot- (5-m) high net that Ned is holding.

Ned reaches into the net and grasps the trapped fish firmly in his hand. Tish swims up next to him with a white board that serves both as a notebook and equipment tray. Like an operating room surgeon, Ned removes a syringe from the tray and expertly draws a blood sample from the damselfish. Then, he places the fish into a plastic bag, hands the bag to Polly, grabs his net, and moves on to the next fish.

Swim into My Laboratory

Ned is a new breed of marine biologist called an *eco-physiologist*, and the work he is doing at Lizard Island is unique. Ned's particular interests are studying the

Ned Pankhurst leads one of the few research teams that studies fish hormones in the animals' natural setting.

effects of *hormones* on fishes and, on the flip side, the effects of fishes on hormones. While most biologists who do work with hormones stick close to the lab, Ned conducts many of his experiments underwater. One of his fish of choice is the spiny chromis—the same abundant damselfish that Brigid Kerrigan works on. Ned wants to trace this fish's hormonal output relative to reproduction and stress.

To do this, Ned makes several trips to Lizard Island each year. He catches fish underwater and draws blood samples from them. Sometimes, he also injects hormones into the fish. The fish use *enzymes* to convert these hormones into other hormones. By measuring the hormone levels in the blood samples, Ned can find out which enzymes are active in a particular fish.

"We want to know the physiological difference between a reproductive, or mature, fish and an unreproductive, or immature, fish," Ned explains. "We've discovered that animals from different locations have different hormone levels, and we think that's related to habitat quality. During the crown-of-thorns invasion around Lizard Island, for instance, we've seen a real degradation of many reefs. If habitat quality goes down enough, many of the fish will stop reproducing and their hormone levels will change.

"We're trying to find out whether we can learn which fish are reproducing and which fish aren't by measuring their hormone levels. If we can do this, we'll be able to go out on a reef and figure out whether it's a good fish habitat simply by catching fish, measuring their hormone levels, and seeing how many of them are reproducing."

Aqua-Stress and Toxi-Stress

Originally from New Zealand, Ned has worked on fish hormones and reproduction for more than 20 years. Much of his work is "pure research"—just wanting to understand how fish reproduction works at a hormonal level. But the work has wide applications for fisheries and aquaculture as well.

"One of the reasons we're fiddling with this," Ned explains, "is because stress management is really important for getting fish and other desirable animals to grow and stay healthy in captivity. By learning how animals respond to stress at the hormonal level, we can understand how to successfully raise these animals for aquaculture."

Ned's research also provides insights into the effects of pollution on wild animals. In many parts of the world, paper mills and other industries discharge toxic "cocktails" of chemicals directly into rivers and lakes. Many of these chemicals mimic animal hormones and may drastically affect the animals' growth, behavior, and reproduction. Ned's work on the reef and in the lab helps scientists understand just how dangerous these pollutants can be and what steps we must take to create a healthy environment.

SEVEN

Crisis and Conservation

THE BIOLOGISTS WHO WORK AT LIZARD ISLAND AND OTHER coral reef research facilities are driven by a fundamental curiosity about marine life and how it works. Their passion comes from wanting to answer hundreds of questions about how animals survive, reproduce, and interact with each other. As the scientists work to answer these questions, they are also collecting information we need to protect Earth's incredible coral reef ecosystems. Never has the need to protect coral reefs been greater.

The world's coral reefs suffered terribly in 1998. Besides increased pressures from pollution, overfishing, and coastal development, many coral reefs experienced the warmest ocean temperatures ever recorded. These warm temperatures triggered a widespread phenomenon called *coral bleaching*. Coral bleaching occurs when corals are exposed to severe stress and lose the symbiotic zooxanthellae from their tissues.

Corals often recover from mild coral bleaching, but severe bleaching causes massive coral death, and in 1998, reefs suffered the most severe bleaching yet.

Reefs in the Indian Ocean, Southeast Asia, the Caribbean, and parts of the far eastern and western Pacific Ocean were especially hard-hit. In some areas of the Indian Ocean, more than 90 percent of the corals died, including huge coral colonies up to 1,000 years old. In Australia, extensive bleaching occurred along a 360-mile (600-km) stretch of the Great Barrier Reef and was reported in many other areas as well. Sea temperatures soared to between 5 and 10 degrees Fahrenheit (3 and 6 degrees Celsius) above normal.

Coral Calamities

The massive bleaching event that occurred in 1998 was only the latest crisis to hit the world's coral reefs. Since people began looking at them 50 years ago, reefs in every part of the world have suffered severe damage, almost all of it from human activities.

Human impact on reefs comes in many forms. One major culprit is coastal development. When people clear land for farms, towns, and resorts, large amounts of topsoil often wash into the ocean. Coral reefs need clear water for their zooxanthellae to make food from the sun. If the water remains muddy for too long, zooxanthellae and their host corals die. Coastal development also leads to another problem—large quantities of sewage, oil, industrial wastes, and fertilizers being dumped into the ocean. These contaminants kill corals and other reef animals.

Overfishing has had a tremendous impact on coral reef communities. In wealthier nations such as Australia and the United States, fishers target sport fishes such as coral trout while divers collect lobsters, conchs, and other desirable species. In poor countries such as the Philippines and Indonesia, people harvest just about everything they can catch. Many of their fishing practices are extremely destructive. Some people set off dynamite and then collect the fish that float to the surface, leaving behind a wreckage of dead corals, fish, and other animals below the surface. Others poison fish with cyanide, while still others use a method called *muro-ami*. In this insidious practice, skin divers drive or "herd" fish into nets by noisily smashing corals with rocks and poles.

Reefs face other threats, too. Divers have cleared many reefs of fish for the live aquarium trade. Other reefs have been dynamited or smashed apart by people searching for cowries and other shellfish to sell to seashell collectors. Boat operators often drop their anchors on living corals, smashing and tearing them apart without regard for the creatures that depend on them. During the Gulf War, many reefs ended up covered with oil, killing them and their many inhabitants.

The Hot Zone

As serious as these threats are, the 1998 bleaching event made it clear that the world's reefs face one danger that may outweigh all others: *global warming*. By now, most of the world's scientists agree that the Earth's atmosphere is heating up. Seven of the ten hottest years in recorded human history occurred in the 1990s. 1998 was the hottest year ever, and 1999 was the fifth hottest on year on record. Most experts predict this trend will continue.

As with other dangers to reefs, human beings are the main culprit. As we burn coal, oil, and natural gas to generate electricity and power automobiles, we release unprecedented amounts of carbon dioxide and

After the 1998 bleaching event, a volunteer diver surveys damage to staghorn corals on the Great Barrier Reef.

other *greenhouse gases* into Earth's atmosphere. We also release greenhouse gases when we cut down and burn the world's forests and grasslands. These gases trap enormous amounts of heat in the atmosphere, preventing it from radiating back out into space. The result is an increase in worldwide temperatures known as global warming.

Even though coral reefs have survived for millions of years, corals themselves live within fairly strict temperature zones. Waters that are just a little too warm cause coral bleaching and death. Many scientists believe that 1998 may just be the first in a series of years that witness damage to reefs on a widespread, unprecedented scale.

The Reefs less Traveled

Despite global warming and other threats, coral reefs survive, and even flourish, in many areas. While most reefs in Southeast Asia have been severely degraded, others in the Middle East, Central Pacific, and Australia continue to thrive. The Great Barrier Reef is one of the survivors.

Why are some reefs doing better than others? One reason is the number of humans nearby. Reefs in heavily populated areas receive more pollution, runoff, and fishing pressures than reefs in less populated areas. "The best management idea we ever had in Australia," biologist David Bellwood says with a wry smile, "was putting the Great Barrier Reef up north and 50 miles (80 km) offshore. That's the main thing that's kept the reef in such good condition. If the reef were next to a major city like Melbourne or Sydney, we wouldn't be talking about reef management right now. We'd be talking about reef regeneration. So I don't think we can compliment ourselves too much on effective management."

"Having said that," David continues, "I have to add that here in Australia—unlike in a lot of other places—we're in a really good position. We can learn about the system and begin actively managing it before we're faced with the crises that the Philippines and other countries now face."

Essential Science

The research David and other scientists are conducting not only provides us with fascinating insights into how coral reefs work, but also gives reef managers the knowledge they need to make wise decisions about how to use reefs without destroying them. Unfortunately, biological research is drastically underfunded and underappreciated in Australia, the United States, and many other countries.

According to Julian Caley, a scientist who works at James Cook University, biological research on reefs is a particularly low priority. "Biologists are considered to be a pain because we don't make any money for anyone," he explains. "Because industry and government can't make a buck out of us, they don't give us much money to conduct our research."

This shortsightedness is especially ironic considering the tremendous economic benefits of a healthy coral reef. One study in the Philippines showed that using a healthy reef without destroying it produces *fifty times* more money than can be earned from exploiting it with cyanide and dynamite fishing.

In Australia, the economic benefits are even more obvious. Millions of tourists travel to Australia every year to dive, snorkel, and fish on the Great Barrier Reef. These tourists spend hundreds of millions of dollars on hotels, food, and entertainment. If the reef is destroyed, that income will be lost, and Australia's economy will suffer. Investing a few million dollars each year to understand how to keep the reef healthy will pay off in hundreds of millions—probably even *billions*—of dollars in benefits down the road.

Reef Warriors

Despite government underfunding, scientists in Australia and around the world are working hard both to understand reef processes and protect reef resources. In 1995, world coral reef experts met for the first International Coral Reef Initiative Workshop in the Philippines to develop global strategies and guidelines for protecting coral reefs. Since that time, reef managers, businesses, nongovernmental organizations, and governments have cooperated on a wide variety of coral reef protection strategies.

Two important new tools for reef protection are Reef Check and the Global Coral Reef Monitoring Network, or GCRMN. Both of

Biologists use standard 1-meter squares to estimate the percent cover of coral and other organisms on coral reefs.

these programs gather up-to-date information about the world's coral reefs. The Reef Check program relies on volunteer scuba divers in more than forty countries to survey the health of coral reefs. GCRMN uses government resources to monitor reefs. Local communities that actually use the reefs are also involved in this program.

In their first 2 years of operation, Reef Check and GCRMN compiled invaluable information about the status of the world's coral reefs. Their first report, *Status of Coral Reefs of the World: 1998*, provided an overview of coral reefs in every part of the world and described in detail the severe magnitude of the 1998 coral bleaching event. The report contained some shocking information.

According to coauthor Gregor Hodgson, "In 1997, the biggest surprises were that serious overfishing of high-value reef animals was widespread and that there were virtually no reefs that were not heavily fished, irrespective of how far they were from human population centers. In addition, marine protected areas were generally no different from nearby unprotected areas, such that management [policies] do not seem to be working to conserve them."

Together, Reef Check and GCRMN provide real data that local, regional, and national governments can use to manage their coral reefs. By involving hundreds of volunteers and local communities, the programs have raised awareness of coral reefs and unleashed an army of "missionaries" to spread the word about the importance of coral reef conservation.

Coral Reef Communication

Scientists and other people who care about coral reefs also work to directly share experiences and information about coral reefs. In

November 1998, more than 300 delegates from 49 countries converged on the small city of Townsville, Australia, within sight of the Great Barrier Reef. The delegates included biologists, natural resource managers, and government representatives. They had all come to attend the International Tropical Marine Ecosystems Management Symposium. The delegates discussed problems facing coral reefs and programs that have been successful in protecting them:

◆ In the Philippines, local villagers have been working with government agencies to regulate fish catches and replant mangroves along the coast. This should increase the numbers of fish available for harvest and prevent coastal runoff that kills corals.

◆ On the Caribbean island of Bonaire, scuba diving has been tightly regulated and dive boats are required to tie up to permanent moorings instead of dropping their anchors on fragile corals. Divers and the public are being educated about the importance of the reef and told not to litter, touch living corals, or remove any reef animals.

◆ In the African country of Tanzania, local peoples and government agencies have worked with international conservation groups to successfully control dynamite fishing in some areas. They have done this by passing new laws and by developing a radio network to help local villagers report violators.

◆ In Australia, the Great Barrier Reef Marine Park Authority is constantly updating its management policies to ensure that the Great Barrier Reef will survive long into the future. It has divided the GBR into different zones. Some zones allow fishing and recreation. Others are set aside for scientific research and conservation of reef organisms and habitats.

The Big Picture

Even in Australia, however, the future of the world's coral reefs will depend on more than scientific research and local strategies. One sad truth is that as long as there are billions of hungry people in the world, coral reefs will be threatened. This can be seen most clearly in countries such as the Philippines, Madagascar, and India, where there are simply too many people and not enough to eat. For coastal peoples in these countries, coral reefs often offer one last chance to feed themselves. Unfortunately, people often destroy coral reefs and their bounty in a last-ditch struggle to get enough food.

Saving reefs will depend on slowing down and reversing population growth so that the world's poor can feed themselves without destroying their environments. It will involve educating people about the devastating consequences of overpopulation, investing in improved worldwide medical services, preventing destructive wars, and using technology that allows us—especially those of us in richer nations—to live without using up so many of our planet's limited resources.

Just as important as reducing the world's population, however, will be reducing the emission of greenhouse gases that cause global warming. "The future of reefs in the short term, I believe, is reasonably precarious," David Bellwood speculates. "The Great Barrier Reef is still not too bad, but global warming could greatly impact it. We can't have the attitude that we'll look after our reefs and the rest of the world can look after theirs. If global warming is coming—and I believe it is—there's every possibility the Great Barrier Reef could be damaged for good."

Protecting the world's coral reefs will depend on weaning ourselves off of fossil fuels and, instead, producing energy from the sun and other cleaner sources. We already have the technologies to do this but have been slow to implement them. Why? One reason is because powerful oil and automobile companies depend on burning fossil fuels to make huge profits. These industries spend a lot of money to block efforts to introduce newer, cleaner technologies. Governments, especially in the United States, Canada, Japan, and western Europe, must do more to promote solar power, mass transit, and better urban planning—actions that will greatly reduce our consumption of fossil fuels.

In the end, protecting coral reefs is not only the challenge of scientists and environmental managers, but of every government and, ultimately, every individual. We need to let our local and national leaders know that protecting our reefs and other precious ecosystems is a top priority—one we are willing to pay for and make sacrifices to achieve. If we act quickly, we can still save many of the world's reefs and provide future generations with a heritage they can be proud of.

What You Can Do

It's easy to blame poor people living in developing countries for destroying their reefs, but the actions of people in developed nations, such as the United States and Canada, pose an even greater threat to reefs in the long run. We buy fish, seashells, corals, and many other products taken from coral reefs. Our automobiles and industries release carbon dioxide and other greenhouse gases into the atmosphere. These greenhouse gases cause global warming, which triggers catastrophies such as the 1998 coral bleaching event.

There are many things that individuals like you can do to help protect our planet's coral reef ecosystems. Some are simple. Others take more thought and effort. They will all make a difference:

◆ Do not collect corals, seashells, sea turtle shells, and other products that come from coral reefs. Do not buy jewelry, clothes, or souvenirs made from these products.

◆ Do not drive somewhere when you can walk or ride a bike instead. If you must drive, try to carpool with other people going to the same place.

◆ Turn off electric lights and electrical appliances when you're not using them. Most electricity is produced by burning coal or oil, a process that releases millions of tons of greenhouse gases.

◆ Remember the consequences of an exploding human population on other creatures and their habitats. Think carefully before bringing a new life into the world.

◆ If you keep an aquarium, only buy fish that are raised specifically for the aquarium trade. Make your fish dealer *prove* that the fish she or he sells are not taken from a living reef.

◆ Write letters to your congressional representatives, senators, and other public officials urging them to spend money to reduce greenhouse gases, increase public transportation, promote renewable energy sources, protect endangered species, and support worldwide efforts to reduce the human birth rate.

◆ When you turn 18, vote for political candidates who support the programs listed above.

◆ Talk to your friends and parents about the threats facing coral reefs and ask them to join you in following the above suggestions.

Glossary

antifouling compound—a compound that is painted on ships or other surfaces to prevent marine organisms from growing on them

aquaculture—the "farming" of aquatic organisms to provide food and other commercial products

asexually—without sex; the creation of new individuals or young by a single parent without fertilization of an egg by a sperm

barrier reef—a long, narrow reef, usually fairly far from shore, that is separated from land by a lagoon or shallow sea

benthic spawner—a fish or other animal that lays its eggs on the bottom of a lake, stream, or ocean

brood—(noun) a group of young that stay together after they are born; (verb) to keep and protect young until they grow large enough to survive

calcium carbonate—the hard substance created by corals and certain other animals; it forms as a skeleton, a shell, or other structure

Cnidaria (nie-DARE-ee-uh)—the group of invertebrates that includes corals, sea jellies, sea anemones, and certain other "stinging" animals

colony—a group of animals of the same species that live together and depend on each other in some way

coral bleaching—an event in which corals lose or eject their zooxanthellae, usually in response to a severe stress

coral cay—a low, sandy island that has been built up by corals. It usually forms in shallow waters.

crinoid—an animal, such as a sea lily or feather star, that is related to sea stars, sea urchins, and sea cucumbers

cross-fertilize—the process of fertilization with an egg and sperm from separate parents

crustacean—a hard-shelled animal, such as a crab, shrimp, barnacle, or copepod

crustose alga—an alga that grows flat and carpet-like, usually over rocks, dead coral, and other hard surfaces

detritus—particles of organic material that come from dead and decomposing organisms

ecophysiologist—a biologist who studies the relationship between an animal's physiology and its environment and behavior

elastomer—a brightly colored paint that scientists use to tag fish and other animals

enzyme—a molecule that acts as a catalyst for biochemical reactions but is not used up itself

fragment—to break off; a form of asexual reproduction in which pieces of an animal break off to form new individual animals

fringing reef—a coral reef that grows right along a coastline

gender-changing—refers to animals, including many kinds of coral reef fishes, that change from male to female or from female to male during their lives

global warming—the increase of worldwide temperatures as a result of the release of greenhouse gases into the atmosphere

gnathiid isopod—a kind of crustacean. Some gnathiids survive as parasites on other animals.

greenhouse gas—carbon dioxide, methane, or another gas that traps heat in Earth's atmosphere

herbivory—the process of eating plants

hormone—a substance that regulates the growth or function of a specific organ or tissue in the body

hybridize—the production of young by two or more parents of different species

imprint—when a young animal learns to recognize and approach an object or animal, usually its mother

invertebrate—an animal that doesn't have a backbone

larva (pl. larvae)—an animal in an early stage of development; it looks and behaves much differently than in the adult stage

larval stage—see *larva*

light trap—a device used to catch fish larvae and other animals that are attracted to lights at night

marine reserve—an area in the ocean that is set aside to protect marine plants and animals

mass spawning—the simultaneous release of eggs and sperm by many species of corals on the Great Barrier Reef and other nearby regions

microbe—a tiny organism that can only be observed with a microscope. Examples include bacteria, viruses, protozooans, and some algae and fungi.

mimicry—when one species (the mimic) evolves to look or behave like another species (the model) and gains some benefit as a result

muro-ami—a highly destructive method of catching coral reef fish by smashing coral reefs with rocks or other heavy objects to create noises that "herd" the fish into nets

mutualism—a relationship between two different organisms that benefits both of them

olfactory—referring to or related to the sense of smell

otolith—a small bone that forms part of the inner ear of a fish

parasite—an animal that obtains its nutrition from the bodies of other, usually larger, organisms. Parasites cause many diseases but are usually not immediately fatal to their hosts.

patch reef—a coral reef that grows up from a shallow sea bottom, usually away from shore

plankton—small plants and animals that float or drift passively in water currents

polyp—a body form found in Cnidaria that consists of a body stalk with a mouth, digestive cavity, tentacles, and often reproductive organs. In many corals, individual polyps grow together in a colony.

post-settlement mortality—the rate or level at which young organisms die or are killed after their larval stage is completed and they settle back down onto the reef or other habitat

reef flat—an area of flat land behind the wave-exposed edge of a coral reef. It is usually covered with large quantities of sand and rubble.

sexual reproduction—the production of young by the joining or fusion of two reproductive cells (usually an egg and a sperm) produced in different organs (usually ovaries and testes)

spawning aggregation—a group of animals that releases eggs and sperm into the water at the same place and time

toxicology—the study of poisons, especially the effects of foreign substances on living things

ultrasonic telemetry—a system for tracking objects underwater by receiving and following sound waves emitted by a transmitting device

zooxanthella (ZOE-zan-thel-a; pl. zooxanthellae)—a specialized dinoflagellate that lives inside the body of a coral, a giant clam, or certain other marine organisms. Zooxanthellae use their host animal's waste products and the sun's energy to make food, which is also used by the host.

To Find Out More

Books

Hundreds of books have been written about coral reefs and the animals that live there. *The Enchanted Braid* by Osha Gray Davidson (John Wiley & Sons, 1998) gives very good overall information on reef biology, the history of coral research, and coral conservation. I also recommend *The Great Barrier Reef* by Isobel Bennett (Lansdowne Publishing, 1981). For incredible underwater images, look at photographer Carl Roessler's *Great Reefs of the World* (Pisces Books, 1992), and if you're especially interested in fish, try *The Ecology of Fishes on Coral Reefs* (Academic Press, 1994), edited by Peter F. Sale.

Two recent publications provide excellent updates on the status of the world's coral reefs: *Reefs at Risk* by Dirk Bryant et al. (World Resources Institute, 1998) and *The Status of Coral Reefs of the World: 1998*, edited by Clive Wilkinson (Australian Institute of Marine Science, 1998). This last title is also available online (see below).

Magazines

Hundreds of recent magazine articles explore coral reef biology and conservation. Some can be found only in scientific journals such as *Marine Biology*, *Marine Ecology Progress Series*, *Conservation Biology*, and *Ecology*, but many popular articles have also been written. A few recent ones that focus on the status and conservation of coral reefs include:

Chadwick, Douglas H. and David Doubilet. "Coral in Peril." *National Geographic*, January 1999, p. 30.

Hicks, Nigel. "Reclaiming Paradise." *Geographical Magazine*, February 1999, p. 26.

Monastersky, R. "Carbon Dioxide Buildup Harms Coral Reefs." *Science News*, April 3, 1999, p. 214.

Morgenstern, Henry Lee. "Clouds over the Coral." *E*, March 1999, p. 36.

Pennisi, Elizabeth. "New Threat Seen from Carbon Dioxide." *Science*, February 13, 1998, p. 989.

Tickell, Oliver. "Coral Grief." *Geographical Magazine*, August 1999, p. 67.

Wilkinson, Clive. "Leave It to the Locals." *New Scientist*, October 4, 1997, p. 47.

Internet Sites

Many excellent Internet sites explore coral reef biology and conservation. A few of the best are listed below.

AUSTRALIA INSTITUTE OF MARINE SCIENCE

www.aims.gov.au/

The site has all kinds of up-to-date information about Australia's Great Barrier Reef. It also features a complete copy of *The Status of Coral Reefs of the World: 1998* online.

THE CORAL REEF ALLIANCE

www.coral.org/

The Coral Reef Alliance is a nonprofit organization dedicated to keeping coral reefs alive. This site offers basic information on coral reefs, conservation news, and various references and links for learning more about coral reefs.

CRC REEF RESEARCH CENTRE

www.reef.crc.org.au/

This site focuses on research into sustainable use of the Great Barrier Reef. It also has information on overfishing, coral bleaching, and crown-of-thorns sea stars as well as links to other important reef-related sites.

GLOBAL CORAL REEF MONITORING NETWORK

www.coral.aoml.noaa.gov/gcrmn/

This site provides the latest information on the status of coral reefs all over the world.

GREAT BARRIER REEF MARINE PARK AUTHORITY

www.gbrmpa.gov.au/

This site offers links that can help you find the answer to just about any question you might have about the Great Barrier Reef or the research going on there. It also includes a variety of activities.

INTERNATIONAL CORAL REEF INITIATIVE

www.environnement.gouv.fr/icri/

This site describes this organization's mission and includes links to other groups working to conserve coral reefs.

REEF HQ (FORMERLY THE GREAT BARRIER REEF AQUARIUM)

www.reefHQ.org.au

This fun new site was developed and is maintained by the world's largest coral reef aquarium. Check it out!

WORLD RESOURCES INSTITUTE

www.wri.org

This site does not focus specifically on reefs, but contains information and links that address the human causes of environmental degradation including global warming, loss of biodiversity, wars, and overpopulation.

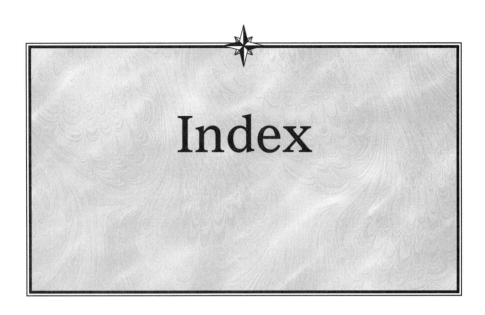

Index

About the Author

Sneed B. Collard III is the author of more than two dozen books for young people, including *Animal Dads*, *Our Wet World*, *Making Animal Babies*, *The Forest in the Clouds*, and *1,000 Years Ago on Planet Earth*. His Franklin Watts titles include *Alien Invaders*, *Birds of Prey*, *Animal Dazzlers*, *A Whale Biologist at Work*, and *Monteverde: Science and Scientists in a Costa Rican Cloud Forest*. *Booklist* awarded *Monteverde* a starred review and described as "intoxicating reading."

Before beginning his writing career, Sneed graduated with honors in marine biology from the University of California at Berkeley. Today, he makes his home in Missoula, Montana, but travels often to research his books and speak to children and educators about writing, science, and environmental protection. To learn more about Sneed's books, school visits, and other activities, check out his website at: *http://www.author-illustr-source.com/sneedbcollard.htm*